The Dread Fishwish

and Other Tales

by George H. Denny

with illustrations by

George Meyerriecks

FRESHET PRESS
Rockville Centre, New York

We wish to thank *Field and Stream* and *Fly Fisherman* for allowing us to reprint stories, and excerpts that have already appeared in their magazines.

ISBN
088395-024-3
Library of Congress catalog card number:
74-79822
Manufactured in the United States of America

Designed by Joan Stoliar

This book is for Mary-Lois, who encouraged, cajoled, and helped me with it and never lost the faith. It is my great sorrow that she could not live to see it published.

Contents

Foreword

A few years ago, when I first considered making these memories into a sporting autobiography, I discussed the idea with an acquaintance who had several outdoor books to his credit. He was not encouraging.

"There's not much market for reminiscenses," he said. "Sportsmen want books telling them where to go and how to do it when they get there."

That just about put the quietus on this effort. I will happily show a small grandson how to drape a nightcrawler on a hook. I might, if pressed by a hunting companion, venture an opinion on whether he was leading those doves enough. Short of that I will not try to sound like an expert. I am perfectly aware that I am not as well informed about some facets of hunting, fishing, and the outdoors than many in whatever audience this book will reach. So if you catch me seeming to give advice, please overlook it. In one or two places I pontificate a bit, but that was on the insistence of an editor who wanted me to appear to be the authority I am not. These stories are to entertain, not instruct.

But in spite of rebuffs, this book refused to go quietly away and expire. It keeps bobbing back up and insisting I do something about it. I had second thoughts. Although I like to read how-to-do-it books by experts, I also enjoy stories that just plain tell about hunting and fishing and the outdoors. I convinced myself there were others like me; enough to make this labor worthwhile. That remains to be seen. But in any case, I have been so fortunate, so happy in my association with nature and the outdoors, that I want to tell about it.

Then, too, my great-grandchildren should know that their great-great-great-grandfather saw the passenger pigeons. I am selfish enough to want them to know it was I who left them the old sporting books and the double shotguns and the split-bamboo fly rods. I want them to enjoy them as I have, and I hope they will care for them and add to them and hand them on to their children. And while wanting them to know about my outdoors and what it meant to me, I have a mortal fear that their outdoors will be one I would rather not know.

In this last thought there is, perhaps, the best reason for a book of this sort. Until now the polluters and poisoners and dam builders have had pretty much their own way. But we have finally realized what they are doing to our world and are beginning to fight back. It will be a long, dirty fight, and it will be expensive. We will have to pay more for many services and products if they are to be provided without damaging our environment. But it is a price that must be paid.

And we will need new weapons to deal with the cheaters who will try to circumvent the anti-pollution regulations we are putting on the books. Fines will not be enough. We must have laws that will enable us to put those criminals in jail. Then their companies will clean up their filth. And if this or any book, even by telling how our outdoors used to be, can in any way reinforce our resolve to intensify the good conservation fight, that is excuse enough for it.

There is something known as sporting license that has nothing to do with the annual permit that allows one to hunt or fish. I refer to the vested right of sportsmen to rearrange matters a bit when necessary to improve a story. There is some of that license in this book. Not much, I promise. Only an inch on a fish here, a couple of yards on a long shot there. Otherwise, except as noted in a case or two, these stories are true.

G.H.D.

Grandfather
and Rabbit Traps
and Passenger Pigeons

My father's father was born on a small southern Indiana farm in 1850, the youngest of eight boys and
three girls. My earliest memory of him is at a
Sunday dinner when he gave me the bright, new Lincoln
pennies that had just replaced the Indian-head design. That
must have been 1910, possibly late in 1909.

Our house was on the edge of the city, surrounded by
woods and fields. During one of those Sunday dinners a few
years later mother complained that rabbits were ravaging her
garden. Grandfather was a tall, courtly man, and I remember
the sharp point of his Vandyke beard as he turned to Father and
asked why he didn't trap the pests. After dinner he showed him
how.

In those days foodstuffs and many other necessities came in
wooden boxes. Our woodshed held an ample supply, waiting to
be stomped into kindling if not put to some other use.
Grandfather chose a sturdy one about two feet square and a foot
deep. Near the garden he laid a floor of planks, so the bunnies
could not dig out, and covered it lightly with dirt. He tacked a
couple of leather hinges to one end of the box and secured them

to the floor planks. Then he showed us how to fashion the figure-four gadget that would drop the box when a rabbit nibbled the carrot impaled on the trigger.

He stood back and admired his handiwork. They didn't have fine wooden boxes like that when he was a boy, he said. They used baskets, and the rabbits would gnaw out if the trap was left untended too long.

The next morning I was out of bed before sunup and woke father to tell him the trap was sprung. Mother said not to hurt the poor thing—she might have a nest of babies somewhere. She needn't have worried; there was nothing in the trap. The carrot was nibbled, but the quarry had somehow escaped. I'm sure it was a fine trap, but in all honesty I can't recall that we caught anything with it.

A little later Grandfather showed me how to make a twitch-up: a copper-wire noose set in a rabbit run and attached to a bent-over sapling so the captive would be lifted from the ground. He was delighted with the smooth, strong efficiency of the copper wire. He had made do with strips of ironwood bark, he said, and it didn't always hold.

My first victim of the twitch-up was a neighborhood cat, caught by the hind legs. We were able to release it, unharmed, with the help of a protective blanket and heavy leather gloves. A few days later I did catch a rabbit in a run in our berry patch. Father showed me how to clean it, mother cooked it, and as we ate it I was as proud as a caveman dragging home his first bear.

There were three big sugar maples on our lot and a couple more in the vacant lot next to us, and one winter Grandfather showed us how to tap them. That project was not a success, however. Boiling down the sap used all our firewood, plus another rick or so that we had to pay good money for. We got less

George Denny

16

than a gallon of syrup. We could have purchased as much for a lot less than it cost us in firewood and labor.

At every opportunity I questioned Grandfather about the hunting and fishing in his childhood. He was vague about the fishing. It was all for food, not sport. They netted creeks and ponds and had neighborhood fish fries. He wasn't sure what sort of fish they took. Bass, he thought, and suckers and catfish. Once somebody caught a catfish in the Ohio River that weighed over 100 pounds. They used a whole rabbit for bait, he said.

About hunting he was more explicit. There were only two guns in the family, and as the youngest he was seldom given a chance to use one. They couldn't afford to waste powder or shot. If anybody fired a gun, he had better bring back meat— mostly wild turkey and now and then a deer and once a little black bear about as big as a sow. They didn't spend ammunition on anything smaller. But his father and older brothers did most of the shooting.

He trapped rabbits by methods described earlier. His quail trap was a basket-like contraption about four feet in diameter, woven from withes and reeds. He would set it on the way to school, in a clearing or on the edge of a grain field. He would sprinkle cracked corn or wheat under the trap and work it into the ground so the birds would have to scratch for it. Then he would lay a trail of the grain out in each direction from the trap. A long string was tied to sticks that propped up one side of the basket. On the way home from school he would sneak up to see if there were quail under the trap, and if so, he jerked the string. Once he got eleven. But often they would clean up the grain while he was in school. One day he got what he called a partridge.

Father explained that he meant a ruffed grouse. I had never

Grandfather and Rabbit traps and Passenger Pigeons

seen one, but I knew about quail. I'd seen them paired in the spring and tried to imitate the clear "bobwhite" whistle. More than once they led me away from nests or young before I learned the reason for their broken-wing act. On the way to school one fall I flushed a big covey in a pear orchard. I walked right into it, and they buzzed up all around me and like to scared me out of my knee britches.

I best remember Grandfather's stories about the passenger pigeons. There were millions and millions of them, he said. Flocks miles long and miles wide. When they appeared folks ran to gardens and grain fields and tried to scare them away. They could destroy a crop in a few minutes.

Nobody wasted powder and shot on pigeons. They caught them in nets and knocked them from roosts with long poles. They salted them down for the winter in kegs. Sometimes the birds crowded the branches so thickly that they roosted on top of each other several layers deep, and many birds were crushed or smothered and could be picked up in the morning. Once they had so many they fed them to the pigs.

He told me a story his mother had told him. She washed a blanket, wrung it out, and flipped it up to shake out the wrinkles. At that moment a flock of passenger pigeons swept by and several hit the blanket and were knocked to the ground.

One day the papers carried a story that a passenger pigeon had died in a zoo in Cincinnati. It was believed to be the last one of the flocks that had once darkened the skies. That was in 1914.

Grandfather snorted. They can't all be gone, he declared. There were too many of them. They'll find some off in the woods somewhere.

But Grandfather was wrong.

George Denny

18

Salt Water

I came to the sport of angling late in life. There were no fishable waters within miles of our house, so I cannot reminisce about padding barefoot down to the stock pond with a can of worms and a willow pole. Wasted years, alas, but I've worked hard since to make up for them.

Martha's Vineyard, with it's great beaches, salt marshes, fish and strange sea animals, was an overpowering experience. We summered at Edgartown when I was ten, and I recall it as a breathless time when I was never able to keep up with all the happenings that needed my attention.

Some of the old whaling ships were still there, either beached or tied to ancient wharves. And a few of the captains that had sailed them around the Horn were still active. One of them lived aboard his ship and fished all day for eels and set out lines for them at night. He kept them in a live-box made from a whale-oil cask. Once a week a dealer bought his catch and shipped it to New Bedford, on the mainland. It was said those eels were the old man's only source of income.

The first fish I ever caught was a cunner from under his wharf. They looked like perch, and the largest I caught was about twelve inches. They liked the shade under the wharf, and the trick was to fish for them when the tide would sweep the baited hook back out of sight. They would attack it there but were clever bait stealers, and it was a rare day when I could take home enough to feed the family. I remember using snails for bait. The tough muscle that attached to the operculum was best.

I watched, fascinated, as the old man caught the eels. I wouldn't have touched one with a boathook. One day I fished too deep and hooked one of the slithery beasts. I was about to cut my line, when the old man saw my confusion, hopped down the ladder like a boy, and had the hook out in a moment. I offered the eel to him, and he was glad to have it. That gift paid off handsomely. He let me use his dory.

I had just learned to swim, but even so I doubt if Mother would have approved. I overcame that possibility quite easily; I didn't tell her. There is no safer craft than a dory. A ten-year-old boy could not possibly capsize one, and I'm sure the captain took that into account when he let me use it. I got in trouble with it only once. A combination of tide and wind was too much for me. The Coast Guard saw I couldn't make it, and they chugged out and towed me back with a stern warning not to trouble them again.

The swordfishermen went out nearly every day. I begged and pleaded, and finally Mother arranged for me to go with one. The captain warned me to keep a safe distance from the coils of rope so neatly stowed in the bow. When he harpooned a big swordfish I saw why. That line whistled out as the fish took off. Small kegs every hundred feet or so kept the line afloat and provided a drag. In a few moments it was over. The fish died

George Denny

from the harpoon wound after a brief flurry. The captain said if he hadn't hit him just right, the fight could have taken hours.

The lookout in the crow's nest soon sighted another fish, and the captain took his place on the bowsprit. This time I shinnied part way up the mast so I could see all the action. The fish was basking in a gentle swell, about a foot under the surface and apparently asleep. Guided by signals from the captain, the helmsman cut the motor when we were about a hundred feet away, and we glided slowly toward the prey. At about thirty feet the fish appeared to take fright, and the captain hurled the harpoon as it began to sink out of sight.

Salt Water

"Got him too far back," he said.

This time the fight took a lot longer, but the fish finally tired and they hauled it alongside, where the captain killed it with a long knife lashed to a pole. I remember that the first fish weighed nearly five hundred pounds—a memorable catch. The second was about two hundred. It was a good day's work, and the captain was pleased. He said I was good luck and gave me a big slab cut from the smaller fish. Mother was pleased with that. She could hardly wait to get home and fry it.

I've eaten swordfish since that time, but none bought at inland fish markets ever tasted half as good. Mother was born and raised in Baltimore, and she had sadly missed fresh seafood. She made up for a lot of lost time that summer. We ate almost nothing but fish, lobster, crabs, and clams.

I furnished some of the shellfish. There were flats where I could wade barefoot at low tide and feel for clams with my toes. The big ones were called quahogs, and Mother made chowder of them. I netted crabs in the marsh grasses. Blueberries grew everywhere on the island, and they made splendid pies.

A few days before our vacation was over, one of the boats brought in a monster swordfish. The crew had fought it all afternoon and most of the night. They towed it into the harbor; it was too large to hoist aboard. The fish's sword was broken. It had charged the boat, and the sword had pierced the hull. As I recall, that fish weighed 1200 pounds and was the largest ever taken out of Edgartown. Newspapers sent photographers for pictures and reporters to get the story of the great battle. That was a fitting end to an exciting summer.

Ten years later I spent another summer not far from there at the Woods Hole Marine Biological Laboratory. I was assistant to my biology professor, who was there on a grant from the Navy to study the toredo, or shipworm, an invertebrate that did

George Denny

much damage to pilings and the wooden hulls of ships. From the beaches at Woods Hole, on a clear day, I could see Gay Head on Martha's Vineyard.

My most vivid memories of that summer are the beach picnics. We boiled lobsters and steamed clams and mussels. It was then that I learned an important lesson about lobster pots. I was fishing with one of the natives, and our skiff drifted by a float that marked a lobster pot. I suggested we haul up the trap and see what it contained. I'll never forget the look of horror that swept over my companion's face when he saw I was serious. If we were caught hoisting a pot, the owner could shoot us and it would be ruled justifiable homicide, he said. It was as bad as horse stealing out West in the old days.

The mussels were my favorite food on those beach parties. They were little black-shelled bivalves about two inches long, and they grew in great clusters on rocks and pilings. We would gather sacksful at low tide, then dig a large hole in the damp sand and build a huge driftwood fire in it. As it burned down to ashes, we threw in a lot of rocks, then banked wet sand around the fire pit and covered the rocks with wet seaweed. On top of that went a wooden cask a little larger than a nail keg. We shoveled more sand around the keg until it acted like a chimney, then filled it with alternate layers of mussels and seaweed. In a few minutes the steam opened the mussels, and we dipped them in butter sauce and downed them. A hungry man could eat several dozen, and the memory of their golden goodness excites my salivary glands today. I remember asking why that delicacy was seldom seen on the fish stalls, and the answer was that they do not keep long. They should be eaten soon after they are gathered and, like sweet corn, the sooner the better.

Salt Water

The First Fly Rod

One day as I was exploring the swampy channel between Big and Little Tippecanoe Lakes I came upon a strange sight. A man was standing in a boat, waving a long rod. I could see the lure wafting back and forth. Now and then he would drop it on the water, let it float for a few seconds, then move it with little jerks. He was moving toward me, and I pushed my boat into the weeds, out of his way, and watched him. In less than a hundred feet he caught a big bluegill and two bass. The last one was hooked on the far side of the channel not

forty feet from me. I saw every detail of that action. He dropped his lure—it looked like a fuzzy, little mouse—within an inch of a lily pad. He left it motionless for several seconds. He gave it a tiny twitch and the bass had it with a fine splash. Then ensued a battle such as I had never seen. It was a husky fish, nearer three pounds than two, and for some time it had it's own way. The long, whippy rod couldn't lift or turn it. It went into the lily pads. He worked it slowly, gently out of that tangle and the fish came across the channel and went around a sunken stob not five feet from where I crouched, entranced. I saw the leader cut into the pulpy wood. He gave the bass line and it went back the way it had come and bored down out of sight in the depths of the channel. He kept the rod bent in a half circle, and in a few more

The First Fly Rod

25

minutes the unrelenting pressure ended the fight. He held it up in his net and smiled at me.

"Gee whiz," I said. "That's a dandy."

"You want him?" he asked. "I have plenty."

I certainly did. I rowed over and he put the fish on my stringer. His stringer held four bass and several bluegills, and one of the bass was larger than the one he gave me. That night I had a fine tale to tell Father.

"That was a fly rod," he pronounced. "It's a very sporting way to fish. It's not easy to learn, either. I tried it once and couldn't get the hang of it. You'd better stick to the casting rod. You have plenty to learn there."

Father was an expert with the casting outfit. From forty or fifty feet he could drop his plug inches from a stump or lily pad every time. And he rarely had the backlashes that took so long for me to pluck out. So when he said fly fishing was too much for him I felt it would be even more so for me. I know now why his first attempt was not successful. Surely the problem was an unbalanced outfit with too light a line. Because of that my introduction to the sport was delayed for a couple of years. But in that time I saw other fly fishermen in action, and I kept pestering Father till he finally bought me an outfit.

The rod was steel and nine feet long. The line was level and enameled. The little single-action reel barely held it and a few feet of backing. But the salesman made sure the line was heavy enough to work the rod. Father was amazed.

"Why it's not so hard," he said, lobbing it back and forth on our front lawn. He subsequently bought a couple of fly rods but never cared for them as much or used them as well as he did the shorter sticks.

The next day Father had to drive up to Monticello on business.

George Denny

"It's right on the Tippecanoe River," he said. "Bring the new outfit. You can try it out for a couple of hours while I see the judge."

It was mid-August, and the river was low and clear. Father dropped me a couple of miles below the town. Just after noon on a hot, still August day would not now be my choice of a time to fish, but I knew no better then. I rigged up with a six-foot leader that must have tested at least fifteen pounds. To that I attached a large Red Ibis wet fly. I wouldn't pick that fly today, under those conditions, but it looked good to me then.

I had practiced for hours on the lawn, and my timing wasn't too far off. I snagged myself in the back of the neck once and tangled the fly in a bush on the backcast. Then I began to get the feel—the quick lift that puts the rod to work. The first strike was from a bass that got into the heavy, bright green weeds that line the channels in midsummer, and I lost him there. A few feet farther down I hooked another and soon landed my first fish on a fly rod. He wasn't quite a keeper, but I hated to put him back after the dandy fight he made on the limber rod.

I came to a stretch with a wide gravel bar on one side and a curving, undercut bank on the other. I waded out until I could get my fly into the deep water. A half-submerged log made a back-water, and it was there that the fly was taken in a fine boil. I knew at once he was a good one. He bored downstream, helped by the current, and I had to give line. I backed out of the water and ran down to the end of the gravel bar, and we fought it out there.

He had already jumped once, a splendid, gill-rattling leap at least two feet high. I could see the red fly in the corner of his mouth. He jumped again, then bored deep and took more line. I suppose it wasn't more than three or four minutes before I began to bring him in, but it seemed a lot longer. Then he saw me and surged away again. Twice more I had to give line as I tried to

The First Fly Rod

27

beach him, and when I finally slid him out on the gravel that bass was completely through.

He was barely fourteen inches long. I'll never know what he weighed as I cleaned him then and there. I had taken several largemouths and one or two smallmouth that were larger, on bait or by casting, but none had ever given me such a battle. When Father honked for me an hour or so later I had one more smallmouth and a large redeye and I was a fly-rod man from that day on.

There were good smallmouth streams much closer to home, so I didn't fish that stretch of the Tippecanoe more than three or four times in the next few years. Then the Army Corps of Engineers dammed it, and that was the end of that rich and lovely length of wadeable smallmouth water, the finest, I believe, I have ever seen. I would like to be President for just one reason: to cut the Army Engineers down to size and make them responsive to the wishes of the people. Some of their water works may be needed, but many are built in spite of the anguished cries of conservationists and sportsmen who see their environment being destroyed. One of their damned dams ruined the finest woodcock cover in the entire nation. I'll tell that sad story later.

Trapping and Slingshots

I was amazed when not one of my three sons showed the slightest interest in trapping. They wanted flying lessons and motorcycles. That's progress, I guess.

In my salad days boys wanted to be either firemen, big-game hunters in Africa, engineers of the Twentieth Century Limited or trappers in Canada. The last was my choice. If truth be known, I still have a faint hankering now and then to snowshoe back to some wilderness cabin and see if I can outwit the wolverine that has been ravaging my trap line. These impulses usually come when I am fuming at the income-tax form and are quickly put aside.

I have already told of efforts with box trap and twitch-up. The next step was steel traps. I worked hard at all sorts of odd jobs, and when I was thirteen, give or take a few months, I had a dozen Newhouse steel traps. They were said to be the best.

At this point I will pause and examine my current feelings about trapping, as compared to fifty-odd years ago. I would no more set a steel trap today than I would shoot a tiger. I have never shot an animal larger than a jack rabbit, and I never will unless I'm starving or in self-defense. And trapping, with its attendant suffering, is worse. If this makes me a soft-hearted old dotard in the eyes of any big, hairy-chested hunters, I am content with the label. How they can slaughter a polar bear or lion and call it sport is far beyond me.

But 'twas not always thus. At thirteen I would have jumped at the chance to slay a deer or moose or just about any wild animal you might name. And as to any outcry about the cruelty of steel traps, I was deaf to it. I was just as much a savage as any boy my age.

As I accumulated my traps I read books on the art. I learned to smoke new traps to kill the scent of steel and man. After the smoking I carried the traps on a pole and practiced setting them by using a stick as a lever so I wouldn't have to touch them, even with gloves. The books pointed out that water sets were the simplest and deadliest, so muskrats were my first targets.

White River was about five miles from our house. Three or four times a week I pedalled out there on my bike. A few times when the roads were icy or snow too high I walked. Finally I caught a muskrat. I remember that it was a humane water set, and the little guy was drowned.

No prime sea otter was so carefully skinned out, scraped, salted, and stretched. It was a fine pelt, dark and lustrous. Even mother, who had seriously questioned the project, was impressed. Father was not.

"No more trapping until you've got that math grade up to passing," he ordered.

George Denny

By the time the math was satisfactory the trapping season was over, and there went my dream of shipping a bundle of furs to the buyers in St. Louis. I don't know how it is today, but then all furs were sent to that city, a hangover from the times when the mountain men brought their winter catch down the Missouri.

After that first winter my enthusiasm for trapping was low. I saw there were better ways to make a living. What revived my interest was a talk with one of Father's friends who had bought a farm and intended to retire there and oversee the production of foodstuffs in short supply because of World War I.

"Something's getting our chickens," he said. "I think it's a mink. The tenant says it's a fox."

The dream of every proper boy in those days was to trap a silver fox. Failing that, any fox was a prize, and a big, dark mink was even better than a red fox. I offered my services. I told him of my fine traps and the muskrat. He laughed.

"I trapped some muskrats when I was your age," he said. "Tried for mink and fox but they were too smart for me. But sure, go ahead and try."

No field marshal ever planned a campaign more carefully. The fall school term had started, and every weekend I bicycled out to that farm. Soon I knew every groundhog hole and muskrat burrow. A creek formed one of the boundaries, and its banks held all kinds of fascinating paw prints. I learned to identify not only muskrat but also possum, skunk, and coon. I asked the tenant why he thought there were fox on his place, and he said he had seen one. There were mink, too. They used down along the creek, and the neighbor boy trapped one last winter, he said.

Ernest Thompson Seton's *Rolf in the Woods* was my Bible. I studied the passage where Quonab taught Rolf how to make a

Trapping and Slingshots

scent that would lure furbearers to their sets, and I would have used that recipe except that it called for beaver castors. Failing that, there were ads in the outdoor magazines that made great claims for various trapping scents. They hinted delicately that they were sex-oriented and would drive furbearers mad. I sent for a bottle, and when it came I opened it in the house. It drove Mother mad.

The opening day of the trapping season found all my traps scented and set. When I ran the line the next morning they were still scented and set except one. A pig had blundered into it and escaped unhurt.

To make it short, I caught one small skunk that first week. Since I didn't know enough about the location of the scent glands to dare skin it, I shamefacedly dropped it down an abandoned well. A few days later my traps began to disappear. I complained to the tenant farmer. It was probably the boy who lived across the creek, he said. Farm boys don't take kindly to city boys moving in on their trapping territory.

So ended my try at trapping; score one muskrat, one skunk, and no return on my investment.

I almost forgot the possum. Grandfather had told me how to get one out of a hollow log. Take a green stick about a half-inch in diameter, he said, and split one end back a few inches and prop the split open about a quarter inch. Poke back into the log until you feel the possum, or other animal, then twist the stick and the fur will tangle in the split and you can drag the animal out. After that I always probed hollow logs, and one day I felt something soft. Grandfather's system worked perfectly, and Mother's large, black cook knew exactly what to do with the little possum. She baked it with yams, and they were delicious, but Mother said the possum was too greasy and wouldn't let us have more than a bite or two.

George Denny

32

In those days a small boy without a slingshot was practically naked. The raw materials for making one were easy to come by; much more so than today. Every carriage house or garage had discarded inner tubes, and they were made of natural rubber. Today's tubes, if you can find any, are made from some sort of synthetic gloop that has about as much elasticity as my aging arteries. The rubbers, a leather tongue from an old shoe, a forked branch, maple by preference, and that's all you needed. Rounded pebbles were plentiful in creeks and rivers.

I'd rather forget some of the things we did with slingshots. We would chose up sides and have battles, and why some eyes weren't put out defeats me. Once I came home with a bloody ear, and when Mother discovered how I got it she confiscated my slingshot. But her memory was short, and I kept my next one hidden in the shed.

We were good with those weapons. Many an English sparrow bit the dust. In those days they were called pests, and the Audubon Society encouraged us to slay them. In truth, not all of us stopped at pigeons and sparrows. Any bird that offered a tempting target was in danger. And dogs that threatened us as we rode our bikes soon learned better.

Jack Malone was the best shot in our neighborhood, but he wasn't in the same class with a small black named Herman who lived a few blocks south. I've seen him hit a pigeon on the wing. He and his even smaller brother, whose name I can't recall, were said to be the inspiration for Herman and Vermin, those characters in Booth Tarkington's *Penrod*.

And now I will make a confession. I shouldn't; it will surely be used against me when I begin to dodder and the family decides it's time to put the old man away somewhere. I have a slingshot, and I practice with it now and then, and I'm pretty darn good with it.

Trapping and Slingshots

It happened like this. A few years ago I had occasion to visit Indianapolis, the city where I was born and raised and had moved from some years earlier. Business completed, I drove out to see the neighborhood where I had lived so many years in a house facing the Butler University campus. I drove through the university grounds and down the hill to the canal where I had fished so often and watched a wood duck raise her broods. The road led through a fine stand of hardwoods—oak, elm, tulip poplar, maple, ash, and beech. I stopped the car to savor the peace and beauty and remembered that near that very spot I had once found a dandy lot of morel mushrooms.

Suddenly I saw treasure. It was a perfect slingshot fork. In my boyhood I had searched for years for a fork of such perfect symmetry, and never found one. Here it was, years too late. And it was white maple, the finest fork wood of all.

Too late? Not so. I marked the spot carefully, drove to a hardware store, and bought a knife. I cut that fork down and carried it triumphantly back to my home in California.

It was then I learned that inner tubes are no longer good for slingshots. After some research I found that surgical rubber is much the best. And my ammunition is not pebbles. It is .45-caliber lead balls cast for the old squirrel rifles. The combination is deadly. It would kill a squirrel or rabbit. I've been tempted a few times, but I find I no longer want to kill anything but game birds and fish.

I've broken that rule just once. One spring a pair of tiny birds—some sort of finch, I think—were trusting enough to set up housekeeping in a bush near the corner of our porch. We watched them incubate four eggs, and when they hatched we put out a plate of crumbs and suet. The next morning I heard their cries of anguish and went out in time to see a bluejay make off with one of the nestlings.

George Denny

34

I used to think it proper to shoot crows because they might eat quail eggs. I thought that mountain lions and coyotes were marauders that must be kept in check. I used to shoot at hawks and owls.

I know better now. The hawk has more right to the quail than I. The coyote that takes an occasional hen pays for it many times with dead rodents. The mountain lion keeps the deer herds healthy. And so on and so on. Man should not butt in on nature's business.

Considering that reasoning, I should have turned my back on the death of the little bird. But I didn't; it was too close to home. When the jay came back for a second helping I was ready with the slingshot. At twenty feet the lead ball nearly tore its head off.

We moved from that house a few days later and not a moment too soon. The children in the block had witnessed the death of the jay. They would look at me and whisper to one another. Once I overheard—"That old man plays with slingshots."

Squabs in the Steeple

Our church was a wonderfully dim, quiet edifice, smelling of sanctity and ancient dust. Grandfather was an elder there and Father a deacon, so I went to Sunday school and church. For several years I was reasonably docile about those Sabbath duties, but there came a time when hunting, fishing, and trapping began to compete with worship, and it wasn't much of a contest. Father was inclined to be stuffy about my derelictions, and strangely, it was Mother who took my side. I remember her words.

"The Lord has had his chance at him. Let the boy go to his outdoor things."

But one thing about the church continued to interest me. The tall steeple was full of nesting pigeons, and they were fair game. They defaced our public buildings, and the city fathers were forever hatching schemes to run them out of town. Now there's a chance for some sport while performing a civic duty, I reasoned.

But our church elders knew a thing or two. The complex of steep steps and ladders that led to the heights of the steeple was a challenge no red-blooded boy could resist. There might be accidents, and the place would be ruled an attractive nuisance in any court of law. The door to the steeple was locked at all times.

I knew better than to make direct inquiry. Father would have forbidden me to set foot in the place. But what the elders didn't know was that Ownie O'Dell, son of the minister, had somehow learned where the key was kept. It didn't take much to persuade Ownie to go pigeon hunting. He was just as curious as any proper eleven-year-old. He showed me where the key was hidden after I promised never to use it without him.

I'm sure that steeple had never been cleaned. Descendants of pigeons that had heard Henry Ward Beecher preach were still adding to the massive guano deposits. In later years when I read of the Augean stables, that church steeple was the first thing that came to mind.

But small boys are not deterred by such trifles, and we worked our way up, by easy stages, to the highest slit window. The view from there was spectacular, but it was the wealth of pigeons that made us feel like foxes in a hencoop. That steeple was a treasure trove. There were plenty of squabs about to graduate into full-fledged birds and dozens of naked nestlings that would soon be squabs.

You don't hear much about squabs these days, but circa 1916 they were expensive luxuries, ranking with terrapin and truffles. They sold for a dollar apiece, or more, if memory serves. Careful harvesting of the crop in that steeple would have assured us steady incomes in the highest juvenile brackets.

Squabs in the Steeple

But we failed to cash in on the opportunity. We were conscious of being not just trespassers, but transgressors as well. If we were discovered up there, we would surely lose privileges. If we sold a lot of birds and came home with money, there would be questions. And so our squab-snatching was limited to a few furtive transactions that netted us very little. My parents enjoyed the two I took home. Father asked pointed questions as to their origin, but I was able to satisfy him with an airy fib about pigeons in somebody's carriage house.

Our last trip to the steeple was on contract. One of our friends had been reading about homing pigeons and had decided to install a loft in his back yard. But when he answered the ads in *St. Nicholas* (for the benefit of you fledglings, that was a children's magazine) he found that the homing strain was more than he could afford. Somehow we convinced him that he could domesticate and train the common wild variety and that we were prepared to supply either adult breeding stock or squabs. He decided on the grown birds, and after some dickering we agreed on eight for a dollar.

That was our sixth or seventh trip up the steeple, and the pigeons were beginning to question our motives. It took us nearly all afternoon to capture eight of them, and we had to cheat a bit on the last one. It was a squab big enough to flap around inside the steeple but afraid to venture outside.

Dusk was deepening as we descended to the church. The door to the steeple was heavy, and it took both of us to close it tight enough to work the lock. I put the sack on the floor and turned to help Ownie. We wrestled the door shut and Ownie turned the key, and as I stooped for the sack I saw the last of the pigeons escape from it. The drawstring at the top had loosened.

We recaptured the squab that couldn't fly higher than the back of the pews, but the rest were long gone. They soared and

George Denny

38

circled, up and up, and finally perched on the great beams just under the roof. At first we were amused, but soon the dreadful possibilities struck us. We could not get those frightened birds down. They would stay up there all night and they would not be continent. Tomorrow was Sunday.

The next morning Ownie told his mother he wasn't well, and she kept him home. I got up before sunrise and went fishing. It took us several days of guarded inquiry to learn what occurred that morning.

Apparently nothing much happened as the worshipers entered the church. A few were seen brushing off their pews and then peering into the dim shadows under the roof. But it was not until Charlie Hansen the blind organist, struck the first thunderous chords of "Rock of Ages" that the action began. Father said, "Seemed like there were pigeons everywhere."

The service that morning was a short one. Ownie and I were never blamed.

Guns

Father wouldn't let me have a BB gun. They are not dangerous enough, he said. They won't hurt very much unless they hit you in the eye, and soon you would get careless in handling a gun, and that's bad.

"I want you be afraid of guns," he said.

He even discouraged me from playing with toy guns.

"It will teach you bad habits," he said. "You must learn never to point a gun at a man unless you intend to shoot him. Play with that cap pistol if you want, but I won't let you have a real gun for a long time after you have stopped pointing toy guns at people."

I stopped playing with toy guns. When I was eleven he brought home a .22 Savage bolt-action repeater. He took me to an indoor range, and we shot at targets until I knew what I was doing. I had tagged along on many rabbit hunts, and he had impressed all the safety rules on me. The rabbit season opened a few days later, and he took me on my first serious hunt.

"I don't expect you to hit one running," he said, "but I'll hold my fire if it's open country, and maybe one will stop and look back at us and give you a sitting shot."

It didn't work out that way the first day. The cover was heavy, and I missed one long chance. Father took over and got three with his shotgun. On later hunts that fall I did get two or three sitting, but I saw that a rifle was no weapon for rabbits and yearned for the day I could have a scattergun.

In the meantime I got in a lot of practice with the rifle. Father belonged to the National Guard, and they sold their members .22 long-rifle cartridges for—hang on—ninety cents a thousand. He brought me home a carton nearly every week. I resold them to my rifle-bearing friends for twenty cents for fifty. That was less than they had to pay at the hardware store, so everyone was happy. I repaid Father, shot all I wanted, and had pocket money for more candy and chocolate-ice-cream sodas than were good for me.

With several hundred round to expend each week I got to be a good offhand shot. Several of my friends had .22s, and every Saturday found us out in the country, plinking away at all sorts of targets. Father had warned me sternly to obey all game laws and not shoot at song birds. I obeyed him, more or less. Most of our shooting was at tin cans or bottles. I remember a dump that had plenty of both. Soon stationary targets were too easy. We tossed them in the air, and after a few thousand tries we could hit them regularly. Any crow or blackbird that flew by was in real danger. I knocked down one crow and more than one blackbird. We were told that starlings were also fair game, but I can't remember hitting any of them on the wing. One farmer gave us permission to try for the pigeons that nested in his barn. He said they carried hog cholera. He wouldn't let us shoot inside

Guns

41

his barn, for obvious reasons, and the pigeons soon learned not to perch on the roof. That left us only wing shots, and we did get two or three that way. I remember thinking how easy it would be with a shotgun.

The next fall, after all that practice, I was cocky enough to shoot at running rabbits. After many tries I got one. I'll remember every detail of that action as long as I live. I saw the rabbit in his form before he jumped. As I took rapid aim he saw he was discovered and took off. I swung with him, and pulled the trigger on his second or third hop. Got him right in the back of the head.

Father saw it. He said, "Humph, that was a lucky shot." But later I overheard him describing it proudly to one of his hunting companions.

My eyes were sharp then. I often saw rabbits before they jumped. Twice I reached down and caught them by hand as they crouched in their forms. That may seem like a difficult feat, but actually it was more a matter of good acting. If I gave the rabbit no reason to think I had seen him, he might not take alarm. I would move to a spot where the high grass hid me from him and could then make a quick stoop and grab.

On my twelfth birthday Father brought home an Ithaca twenty double, Serial No. 263042. The barrels were 28 inches—right, modified; left, full choke. It weighed an ounce under six pounds. It was a Field Grade, and in that year of our Lord 1917 it cost $39.50.

Father took it out of the canvas case, put it together, glanced through the barrels, clicked it shut, and handed it to me. I immediately forgot every safety precept he had drilled into me. I whooped with joy, flipped up the safety, pointed the gun out the window in the general direction of my sisters playing on the lawn, and pulled both triggers.

George Denny

Father said, "I see you're not quite ready for a shotgun," and took it from me and locked it up. He locked my rifle up too, but relented and let me use that during the hunting season a few months later.

On my thirteenth birthday he brought forth the shotgun.

"What did you do wrong a year ago?" he asked.

I'd had plenty of time to ponder that question.

"I pointed it at people and snapped the triggers on empty chambers."

"That's right," he said, handing it to me, "and now you know what happens when you break the rules."

And so, after a bad start, began my association with the shotgun I shoot today. From the first day it fit me perfectly. The drop was right, the stock length was right. It aimed like pointing a finger. And thanks to all the practice with the rifle, I shot well with it the first time I pulled trigger. That was a few minutes after the second giving. We drove out to the edge of town, and Father threw clay pigeons from a hand trap. I broke three or four, and it wasn't until he threw me some low, twisty chances that I missed. I had perfect confidence in the gun that first day and still have. In the fifty-odd years I have shot it I have tinkered with it only twice. After a couple of seasons it became plain that the choke barrels were not best for our bobwhite quail. I was a snap-shooter, and too often I mangled birds. Then, too, much of the shooting at singles was in heavy brush where I had to crack down at ten or fifteen yards or lose the chance. I explained all this to the gun-smith and he nodded wisely and said he knew exactly what was needed.

He cut two and three-eighths inches off the barrels, and at first I thought he had ruined my little sweetheart. But he knew his business. The right barrel is nearly wide open. I have dropped incoming doves with it at ten yards, and they weren't damaged. I

Guns

don't try to reach out very far with that barrel, but just last week, in the middle of the dove season, with birds flying high and scared, I brought down several at thirty yards. The left barrel is modified choke and reaches a bit farther.

For years I have wondered why so many of my hunting friends and companions were continually trying out new guns. Father was an example. He was never quite satisfied with the shotgun he was currently using. He changed and traded every year or so, and as a result he never had a fair chance to get properly acquainted with any of them.

Now I understand that I was just plain lucky that my first shotgun suited me so well. I wouldn't sell it for any amount or trade it for a Purdey or Parker. I would be lost without it. I have two other shotguns, both doubles, of course. I'm one of those cranks who think repeaters and automatics should be outlawed, and that if you can't get your bird with two shots, you don't deserve it.

One of the others is an L. C. Smith twelve. I bought it because it feels and handles exactly like the twenty. The drop and stock length are identical to the twenty, and I knew I should have a twelve for ducks and geese. The third one is a sixteen gauge made in the twenties in Frankfurt by a German gunsmith named Wilhelm Collath. I can't shoot it well, and I knew I couldn't when I bought it. The stock is a hair too long, and the drop a mite too little. I bought it because I couldn't resist the exquisite work-manship. The engraving alone couldn't be done for a thousand dollars today. The checkering is deep and fine. In deference to cold fingers, the trigger guard is made of horn. The stock wood is beautiful. But because it is a German gun, I was able to buy it for two hundred dollars. A Parker of comparable grade would cost at least two thousand. It doesn't make sense.

George Denny

44

I take that lovely thing out of its case and caress it and admire it from time to time. It's a shame it's not in use, and I would give it to one of my sons if it fit them. It doesn't, but there are grandsons on the way, and one of them will surely grow into it.

I've had the L. C. Smith for ten years. It shoots beautifully. It fits me exactly. I should take it on any hunt for ducks or geese or when the smaller birds are flushing wild or flying high. But I don't. I look at them both, the twelve and the twenty, and I take the little gun. It's like fishing for trout. I know if I use a 6X leader, it will probably break in any big fish, but I'd rather hook one and lose it than not have the chance.

The twenty has served me too well and too long to be left at home, even if it means I can't take some shots that are too long for it. I'd rather wait for ones in its range and, know it will handle them perfectly if I give it the chance.

Trout

I caught my first trout from the Sturgeon River in northern Michigan. I was a summer guest there of Dan Layman, whose father, the doctor, was a devoted trout fisherman. I was fourteen, and my angling had been limited to bass and panfish. I used the same dapping technique I had learned on my Indiana lakes and rivers. I crouched back from grassy banks, lowered the grasshopper near them, and listened for the rise. After a few tries it came, and I derricked an eight-inch trout back into the meadow.

Is that all there is to this trout fishing? I thought. Nothing to it. And a few minutes later I caught another one. Then the gods of the angle awoke and frowned, and I caught no more trout that day or for many days to come. In addition to hoppers I tried worms, grubs, crickets, wet flies and streamers with and without a spinner. I'm sure my clumsy thrashings with the heavy steel fly rod scared the bejasus out of those fish. I watched the doctor and other experts and came to realize that my efforts were an insult to the sport. I began to hope for the day when I would be properly equipped. About ten years later that dream was realized. A relative died and left me his four-ounce Cross rod, Hardy reel, and double-tapered Halford line.

Incidentally, some old-timers may be interested to hear that the silk Halford line—now at least fifty years old—is still in good condition. For years I neglected to take it off the reel in the winter, but it didn't begin to get tacky until this spring. I caught that in time and expect to use it many more years. I have never found one of the new plastic lines that feels as good or drops a fly as softly. That statement may bring cries of outrage from the line manufacturers, but that's how it seems to me, and while I'm putting forth my cranky old ideas I may as well be hung for a sheep as a goat. I declare that no glass rod I have ever handled has felt as good to me as my split-bamboo sticks. If this be treason, make the most of it.

It was Chick Moores who finally took me to the Michigan trout streams again. He was a dedicated angler. I'm sure that if bass or trout were not to be had, he would have fished for carp or catfish. As we flyfished for bass in the Indiana streams he would rhapsodize about the thrills and skills of trout fishing. He showed me his flies—tiny, delicate things, some tied on hooks so small I wouldn't believe they would hold a decent fish. And his trout rod—I think it was a Thomas—was only seven feet long and weighed barely three ounces. I could see that my big bass rods and what went with them would be as much out of place on a trout stream as an ax at an appendectomy. And I think he painted a bit too vivid a picture of the artistry and intricacy of the sport; he made me wonder if I could compete in that arena. And so, for several years, I found reasons why I couldn't go trout fishing with him.

But when I inherited the Cross rod I was anxious to try it. Chick took me to the Baldwin district in west central Michigan. The fishing camp was a hodge-podge of ancient cabins, some log, with stove heat and outdoor plumbing. It was run by a little Englishman named Dave Kennedy and I'll never forget his in-

Trout

47

terminable tales about the time he served in the British "nivy." The food was good and the meal times flexible for the whims of trout fishermen, and best of all in those Depression days, the rates were reasonable. One dollar and a half a day for bed and board.

Within five miles of that camp, as the crow flies, there were at least fifty miles of trout-fishing water. The nearest was the Little South, about two hundred yards to the east. To the north about a quarter of a mile the big river, Pere Marquette, flowed west under the highway bridge. It had been formed not far to the east by the confluence of the Little South and Middle Fork. Another mile or so farther north the Baldwin angled under the highway on its way to a junction with the Pere Marquette.

Those four rivers wandered all over the place, loop after loop. Many of those loops would cover a mile or two or even three and then come back to within a few yards of the start. The net gain toward Lake Michigan might be fifty yards or less. There were places where we could park the car, fish upstream for two or three hours, and come back to within sight of the car without getting out of the water. One day I saw an aerial photograph of that country, and it looked like a basket of snakes. It was then that I made the estimate of fifty miles or more of fishable water within five miles of camp.

I had fly-fished for bass enough to know how to throw a line, and the outfit I had inherited was well balanced. On the way up we stopped at Grand Rapids and Chick masterminded the purchase of flies, leaders, tippets, and the like. On the first morning, he took me to an open stretch of the Baldwin and showed me a few dry-fly tricks. He demonstrated the hook cast that brings the fly over a rising fish ahead of a leader. He showed me how to drop a fly in a backwater with loose loops of leader that let the fly float without drag for a few seconds. The past

George Denny

master at this last operation was and probably still is Bill Lawrence, who owned and operated Hot Creek Ranch, above Bishop, California, for so many years. I'll have more to say of Bill and Hot Creek later.

One of Chick's instruction casts brought a rise, and he netted a small brown. There were a few rises, and I cast to them, clumsily, I'm sure, but after a few tries the rhythm came, and the fly began to land softly and float convincingly. I remember that it was a gray hackle. On the first rise to it I stared stupidly for a long second, then struck too late. The second rise was a good fish, and I hit so hard I broke in him. While I was tying on another fly and anointing it from my new, red tin of Mucilin, the rise became general. Circles were everywhere. In the next twenty minutes I netted two small keepers, lost one good one in a tangle of roots, and released a couple that weren't quite old enough. Then the rise stopped as if a valve had been turned, and the next half hour brought nothing. I sat on a log and cleaned my fish. Chick joined me and showed me how to open the stomachs and see what they were taking. He floated a black, compacted mass in water cupped in his palm and probed it with a splinter. The mass separated to show some flies, a few small beetles, and a lot of nymphs.

"It's usually like that," he said. "Mostly bottom food. It's not hard to catch them when they're rising to fair-sized flies, but that isn't often compared to the time they spend feeding under the surface. Getting them then is what separates the men from the boys."

I've thought about that statement many times, and I subscribe to it absolutely. I'll never cease to thrill to a rise to my carefully presented dry fly, but it's a greater satisfaction to drop a tiny nymph above a bulging fish, try to guess the nymph's position as it drifts back, then lift and connect when you see (or imagine that you see) what Skues called "the little brown wink in the water."

And so began my adventure into trout fishing, the sport that I sometimes think has given me the greatest satisfaction of them all. I'm glad I qualified that statement because in truth I should not try to grade my outdoor activities. I like best what I am doing at the time—hunting, fishing, hiking, or just sitting on a log and waiting for the wild things to forget I'm there. And increasingly I find it doesn't take a full bag or creel to make a rewarding day.

I went back to those Baldwin waters twice more with Chick that season, and the next year we went up for the opening, taking with us Billy Sully, an electrical engineer who was mistrusted by all our wives. The reason for that was simple. He had discovered a way to make a good living by working at his trade about one week in every month; certainly not more than two. The rest of the time he fished and hunted. A bachelor with no ties, he was constantly seeking hunting and fishing companions and did not hesitate to recruit his married friends for a sporting weekend, or longer. Wives cringed when he phoned. Mine would hand me the phone and say in worried tones,

"I think it's Sully. Remember our bridge party tomorrow."

At this point I will make plain where my wife stood in regard to my love of hunting, fishing, and the outdoors in general. Some are blessed with helpmates who like those sports and accompany their men on outings. Not I. I was blessed with a wife who would not go hunting or fishing with me if I begged. She preferred the home. And not once in more than forty-three years of marriage did she enter any serious objection to my preoccupation with the outdoors. Let's hear it in her own words. The following is a guest column she wrote for me when I was Outdoor Editor of an Indianapolis newspaper.

George Denny

50

"There are things my mother should have told me; things every young girl should know about the male urge to fish. None of my family were angling addicts and I had no warning of events to come. At first I spoke smilingly of my husband's 'fishpoles' and the 'tin box with the stuff in it.' I soon learned they were rods and tackle box, to be handled with reverence if at all.

"I made one attempt to clean out the closet full of gear, old hats and ragged jackets. Just one.

"One eerie morn my spouse shook me awake, bellowing, 'Where's my dry fly dope?'

"My ignorance of piscatorial parlance was so abysmal I thought he said, 'Where's my dry fly (comma) dope?' I was cool for days.

"I learned to leave his things strictly alone. I can't say the same for him. Fancy feathers have been filched from my hats to make flies. My best manicure scissors keep finding their way into his tackle box. Once fur from a neckpiece was needed to make an important lure.

"For years I have played second fiddle to fish. I have seen strong men literally aquiver with anticipation at the start of a fishing trip. I have seen them return, dithering over a trout that wouldn't begin to feed the family, but that fish was solid gold because it bit at a three-ounce Coachman, or something.

"No, I'll never understand it, but it's good to know that when the master of the house is gone for several days he is pursuing a bass or a bluegill, not a blond or a bottle. And in spite of the things mother didn't tell me I will misquote Voltaire to say, 'I don't comprehend my husband's fishing but will defend to the death his right to it.' "

Trout

More About Trout

In those years of fishing the Baldwin district—the learning years—I had the great good fortune to meet that fine gentleman and superb trout fisherman, Ralph Widdicomb. He remembered when there were grayling in Michigan, before the turn of the century, and had fished for them and trout all his life. He built a cottage on the Pere Marquette River, and when he retired from his lumbering and furniture-making activities he spent most of his time there. It was on a sharp bend of the river, facing a long, straight run that looked as though it would surely undercut the porch sooner or later. Below the bend was the Clay Hole, far too deep and slippery to wade. And from its depths, on warm summer nights, rose huge trout that sucked and slashed at moths or other surface prey. Ralph said at times they sounded like pigs wallowing.

Chick Moores had courted Ralph's daughter some years earlier, and though that romance didn't jell, his friendship with her father continued and deepened. Ralph had introduced Chick to trout fishing, and from Chick's account I envisioned a wizard whose wand was a trout rod. I was not disappointed. He was tall and spare, with slow speech and a quick smile. And I believe he was the finest trout fisherman I will ever know.

The first thing I noticed was how slowly he fished. Up to then I had been splashing along as though the season would end in half an hour and I had to cover all the water possible in that time. Ralph would take five times as long on the same stretch. I made careful note and tried to slow down but I know I still work too fast.

Ralph preferred the dry fly and would sit on his porch, reading, until he saw rises. His rod was rigged, ready and resting on pegs over the screen door. He wore his fishing hat, decked with dozens of flies, at all times. Chick said he slept in it, and he didn't deny the charge.

So when a rise began he would step into waders, sling on his creel, pluck the rod from over the door as he left the porch, and start fishing. And he would take trout from spots I wouldn't have bothered to try.

I asked him about nymphs and wet flies. Properly handled they would take more fish than dry flies, he said. That stood to reason, since there was always more food under the surface than on it. The deadliest method was to fish them upstream on a slack line, but it was also the most difficult. One had to develop a sort of sixth sense to know when to tighten, he said. Years later I read the same advice in G.E.M. Skue's books.

On that first afternoon we sat on his porch and talked and watched the water. Fishing had been good that spring, Ralph said, though Chick and I hadn't found it so. We told him where

More About Trout

we had fished and with what flies. He suggested a couple that had served him well. He predicted that there would be a few mayflies that evening. There had been a small hatch a few miles downstream the evening before and they would work up, he thought.

He was right. A few big mayflies appeared that evening; very few. But the water surged and churned with trout. I'll never forget that frantic evening. Time after time Chick and I floated mayfly imitations over those feeding fish. Not one would have them. Not until the activity was over, after more than an hour of frustration, did Chick suggest an answer.

"You'll notice we saw only a few flies on the water and the trout weren't taking them," he said. "I'll bet they were nymphing—catching the larvae before they made it to the top and hatched. Those fish weren't breaking the surface; they were bulging. We should have tried big nymphs."

We checked with Ralph the next morning. He verified Chick's conclusion. He had taken one four-pound brown and several two pounds or more, all on a mayfly with the wings cut off and fished wet. He said that on a sparse hatch like that the fish were able to intercept most of the larvae before they got to the top. On a heavy hatch they would take a few nymphs at the start; then come up for the hatched flies on the surface.

We asked what to expect that evening. He said if the hatch was as heavy as he thought it would be, he wouldn't wet a line. He might throw them the nymph a few times at the very start of the rise, but when fish began to take from the surface, he would retire. There would be a thousand natural flies to his one artificial and what odds were those?

He was right again. We followed his advice and each took a good trout on a nymph at the very start of the rise. Then the water was covered with the big flies, and the surface boiled. We

George Denny

54

changed to surface flies and kept trying, but it was no good. There were a hundred flies to every fish and a thousand to one to our artificials. As it got darker we could not always see which fly was ours and which the natural, and we were striking at any splash that looked close. Chick caught one unlucky small fish. I didn't have a touch, but it was a memorable evening for me because the one I took at the start of the rise was fourteen inches; my best trout to that time.

Chick blamed himself for not recognizing the need for a nymph when trout were bulging the night before. He had seen a couple of mayfly hatches, but none so sparse, when only a few flies made it to the surface. We should have made a killing, and he'd know what to do the next time, he vowed.

I think that trout fishing goes beyond all other sports in intricacy of design and complexity of pattern. Its mastery passes beyond things teachable and understandable into a region of instinct, feeling, or sixth sense. The fundamentals, the mechanics, are not hard to learn. After that there are the obvious lessons, like the one we learned that evening of the sparse mayfly hatch. But from then on it's a matter of experience; trying, observing, experimenting, and putting everything together; things so subtle and intangible there is no way to describe them or pass them on.

It took me years to learn that last. For a while I pestered Ralph Widdicomb. I watched him fish. I asked him to watch me fish and tell me what I was doing, or not doing, that made the difference in our results. There must be some little trick. . . .

He was patient with me, but he couldn't help, and he told me so. Just keep fishing and observing, and you'll pick it up, was his reply.

That same year I also met and fished and talked trout with Rugee White, brother of Stewart Edward White. He had been fishing the Baldwin-area waters for about twenty years. He knew Widdicomb and agreed with all he had told me.

"I'll give you an example," he said. "You know the pool below the High Banks. There's a little backwater behind the stump near the tail of the pool. There are always good fish in that spot and I tried for them for years with never more than a short rise. Then last summer I began to take them out of there. Now I can almost always take a fish there when they are rising. I can't see that conditions have changed and I give you my word I haven't the faintest idea what I'm doing now that I didn't do in all those earlier years."

We were quiet for a while, pondering the mystery of it all. Then he said,

"Here's another one for you. You know the long riffle above the Clay Hole. Big browns come up from the pool to feed there nearly every evening. But to the best of my knowledge no one has even taken one from there except Ralph Widdicomb. I've watched him fish that spot for ten years. I've studied every move he makes. I've tried for them twice as hard as he and never had a rise. He's tried to show me but either he can't explain or I can't learn. Now, why is that?"

I couldn't answer him then, but I know now. Ralph had been fishing forty years to Rugee's twenty.

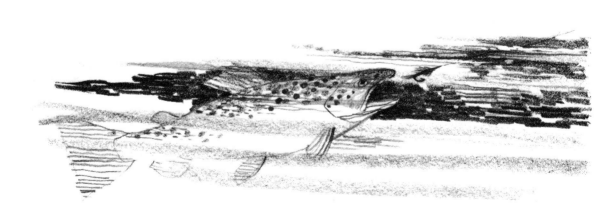

Idaho

In 1925 I spent the summer in Idaho with my golfing and fishing companion George Green. Our friend Hope Pfafflin had a cousin who lived in Lewiston. She invited Hope to spend the summer there and told her to bring boys. There were lots of cute girls, she said, and not enough escorts.

I'm sure there were some romances and exchanges of tender words that summer. There had to be in that lovely country with all those moonlight picnics on the banks of the Clearwater River and elsewhere. But sadly, I can't recall much about the girl I was paired with on those outings. She was cute, I'm sure, but I had seen a lot of girls and never a moose. It's the moose I recall in somewhat more detail.

The train that took us from the main-line junction on a leisurely, winding way down to Lewiston was out of the Gay Nineties, or earlier. The little steam engine had one of those bulbous smoke stacks. It pulled two cars—one for freight, baggage, express and mail, the other for passengers. That was a wooden coach with red-plush seats, a wood-burning stove, and a row of coal-oil lanterns swinging over the aisle.

A few miles of that trip were along the Clearwater River, and it was there I saw my first moose. He was up to his withers in a pool, chomping water weeds that dripped from his big jaws. The train disturbed him not at all. He eyed us placidly as we chuffed by. The engineer saluted him with a couple of steam-whistle toots that he acknowledged with a twitch of his big ears. It was a boy moose, with antlers about half ready for the confrontations of the mating moon.

I recall one more incident on that train trip. We stopped by a water tank on the edge of a small town. The engineer climbed up and lifted back a hinged cover on top of the tender. The fireman swung a big spout out from the side of the tank, and the engineer centered it over the opening. The fireman reached up, took a high hold on the rope, and jerked down with all his might. Water gushed from the spout. Could that explain the term "jerkwater" as applied to a small town?

The best part of that vacation was at the end, when we spent ten days at a sheep ranch on the Salmon River, about eleven miles upstream from the tiny town of Riggins. That's the spot where the float trips end. Those trips are fairly common these days, but in the Twenties they were considered highly hazardous and few dared risk them. There was no road to the ranch; we went in on horseback.

The rancher's name was Gold, and he couldn't have been a finer host. Just once did he tear into us, and with reason. On the third or fourth day of our stay we climbed far up the steep mountainside until the big river looked like white-and-blue wool yarn below us. There, in a thoughtless moment, I pried loose a big boulder and started it down the slope. We watched in fearful fascination as it gathered speed and knocked loose other rocks until several or more were crashing toward the river. I realized at once that I had done a stupidly dangerous thing.

George Denny

58

When we returned that evening Gold was waiting for us, and he was furious. He let us have it approximately as follows:

"You boys are new out here so I'll give you the benefit of the doubt. I got to figure you started that rock slide by accident because not even the damndest kind of a damn fool would do it on purpose. You just be damn sure there's no more accidents. You climb careful after this."

We learned later that one of the hands had been building a holding pen up river, and one of the rocks had barely missed his tethered horse. He came back, boiling mad, and threatened to thrash us both within an inch of our lives, and at first Gold was almost ready to help in that project.

That Salmon River country was a frontier in those days. There was talk about a strange happening called Prohibition in the world outside, but it meant little to those ranchers. They had been making their own whiskey long before Volstead tried to dry the country. Every ranch had a few acres of corn, and it wasn't all for stock feed. Not every ranch had a still; usually several families gathered each fall for the annual whiskey-making. The raw product was faithfully laid down in charred kegs and never consumed until it had some years.

At one ranch we visited, the still was in plain sight in an open lean-to. I asked the owner what would happen if a Federal man came by. He smiled and allowed as how he didn't expect that to happen.

"They wouldn't bother us back in here," he drawled.

On our return to Lewiston I reported that remark to a deputy sheriff. He agreed that the rancher was probably right. He said the last raid in that Seven Devils country was about five years earlier. Two Federal men went back in, destroyed a still, arrested the rancher and his son and started out with them. When they camped that night the rancher's friends came and

Idaho

59

took over. They threw the revenuers' guns and other gear in the river and ran their horses out of sight. They warned them not to bother honest farmers any more and said next time they would get rough. Then they took their boots and socks and turned them loose to hike out twenty miles, barefooted.

Our stay on the Salmon River was climaxed by the early fall get-together of the valley ranchers and their herdsmen, who were bringing the flocks down from the high summer range. That year they gathered at the Gold ranch. The boss man put us to work.

"We'll need a big mess of frying-size trout and a couple dozen blue grouse for the party," he said. "Can you handle those two chores?"

We could, with pleasure, but how about the closed season? How about a hunting license? We had fishing licenses but hadn't planned to stay long enough to hunt.

The big man smiled. "Don't worry," he said. "No seasons or licenses back in here. We take what we need, and we don't waste any."

A small stream flowed past the ranch house on its way to a junction with the big river. The pools were full of trout that averaged about eight inches. I don't remember any longer than ten. When the Golds wanted fish they netted out a pool or two. He offered us the net, but we tried to make some sport of it. We went after them with fly rods and grasshoppers.

Trout in the pools near the house were a bit scary, so we hiked back a few rods to some pools that had probably never been fished. Honestly, it wasn't much sport. Those uneducated trout grabbed the bait the instant it hit the water. They kept after it as long as there was a fragment of 'hopper on the hook. They even struck the bare, shiny hook a few times. We kept them alive in burlap sacks and delivered about eighty of them to

George Denny

60

Mrs. Gold. She put them in a pool in the springhouse, to be netted out as needed.

What kind were they? You've got me. In those days I didn't know *irideus* from *clarkii*. I think they were rainbows, possibly small steelhead, but they may have been cutthroats.

Why didn't we go down to the Salmon River, not an eighth of a mile from the house, and catch some of the big trout and salmon it held? I'll tell you why; we were afraid to fish that wild water. We tried it the day after we arrived at the ranch. I rigged my five and one-half ounce rod with a tandem spinner that had taken a lot of bass back in Indiana. I flipped it into a backwater that was more placid that most of the liquid scenery thereabouts. On the second cast something engulfed it and swam out into the current. I had never felt such ponderous power at the end of a line. There was no tugging or thrashing; just a steady surge. My Indiana bass had never demanded much backing, and what little I had was soon gone. I pointed the rod at the fish and clamped down tight. I was lucky. The break came at the leader.

George wasn't so fortunate. Whatever it was that took his spinner just kept going with leader, fly line, and backing. It jumped once, and was at least two feet long.

I rigged up again with a lighter leader point, to insure the safety of the rest of my tackle, and a small streamer fly. But I made the mistake of trying to wade out a few feet to reach an eddy behind a boulder. I slipped, and the current grabbed and tumbled me. I was lucky to scramble ashore a few yards down, soaking wet, bruised, and without my hat.

That was enough for the day. We did try the big river gingerly another time or two, and George caught a fifteen-incher. But it was plain that our tackle wasn't adequate for those big fish in that fierce water.

Now for the blue grouse. On the day of the party we were

Idaho

61

underway at daybreak. Our destination was a spring about two miles upriver and a quarter mile up the mountainside. There was very little flowing water; it was a seepage that extended across the face of the slope for about three hundred yards. It was bright green in contrast to the dusty gray of the rest of the landscape. Berry bushes flourished there, and they attracted the grouse.

George had a bolt-action .22, and I had my twenty double, and we each had a sack for the game. We had scouted the place once before and marveled at the numbers of birds, never thinking we would have a chance at them. As we approached we saw grouse dropping in for breakfast. Some came from across the canyon. At first they were rather tame. George shot two sitting at close range before they began to spook. I dropped one on the wing as it started across the gorge. I killed it not ten yards out, but by the time it stopped rolling it was thirty yards down the slope. I retrieved it and climbed back. George dropped another, and I missed an easy double. Then I hit one that towered and dropped at my feet, but the next one tumbled far down the slope. By the time I found it and was back on the firing line I was sweating heavily.

In an hour we had twelve birds, and I was panting from the downing and upping after each kill. One cripple fluttered nearly to the river's edge, and it was many weary minutes before I collected it and struggled back. George offered to exchange weapons, and I gladly accepted.

We reached the end of the seepage and started back, but by then the birds were too wary to give me a chance at a sitting shot with the rifle. George got a fine double with the shotgun and had to go far down the slope for one of them.

"This is no good," he panted. "Let's hide in the bushes and take them as they come in."

Idaho

That was a fine idea. We took turns with the shotgun and got the rest of them as they slanted in on set wings. One cripple had to be chased a few yards, the rest dropped in our laps.

Blue grouse are big birds, and those twenty began to feel like that many turkeys as we wrestled the sacks down slippery slopes. We delivered our load at about eleven o'clock, and I had never been so leg-weary, sweaty, and hungry. We were too exhausted to eat, so Mrs. Gold told us to take a nap and save our appetites for the big feed later in the day.

The dinner bell woke us at midafternoon. We put on clean shirts and went to the orchard, where tables were laid and barbecue fires burned. I was so hungry I felt lightheaded. The clans had gathered. Wives and daughters scurried around adding dishes to tables already close to collapse from their loads of food. The men were clustered around the keg of whiskey.

Now I will tell you what food there was for us that afternoon, and I won't blame you if you don't believe me. Five families, eight or ten herders, and George and I made more than thirty hungry people, and the womenfolk had been readying that feast for many a day. A couple of weeks later George and I realized we had seen some sort of culinary history made, so we sat down and listed all the dishes we could remember. I found that list in some old papers recently, and it triggered these memories. I'm sure we forgot some of the dishes, so the following menu is not complete.

The main meat course was a variety of cuts from a fat little spike buck brought by a neighbor. Slices of the fried liver were especially prized. There were lamb roasts and lamb chops. Another neighbor brought two of his barnyard geese and a dozen wild ducks. Our blue grouse were popular, and the trout were being fried and delivered in relays and eaten like crackers. Mrs. Gold opened several jars of bear meat put up the year

George Denny

64

before. It was a bit strong; the only dish I didn't like. There were a couple of hams and many kinds of home-made sausage. There were fillets of smoked salmon, and a small pig was spitted and turning over a fire.

The unsalted butter was home-churned. There was a big round cheese, white and soft, like jack cheese. Each table held a large bowl of cottage cheese, and one of them was topped with a huge dollop of jam—the first time I had seen that delicacy.

My memories of the vegetables are not so sharp, since I had little time for them. Potatoes, fixed several ways, with plenty of gravy both white and dark. All the usual root vegetables like beets and turnips and such. Little wild onions too strong for me. Stuffed green peppers. Hot pepper sauces. Tiny summer squash in butter sauce. Peas and several kinds of bean dishes. A sort of pudding made of pumpkin or squash, with a sugary crust.

Two kinds of bread, yeast and salt-rising, both hot from the ovens. One of the girls kept the biscuit trays filled.

To quench thirsts there were two kinds of home-made wine, coffee, milk topped with yellow gobs of cream, buttermilk, and a cider that was turning fast. It tingled the tongue.

But it was with the jams, jellies, preserves, condiments, and desserts that the women outdid themselves. There were dozens of jams and jellies, made from every available fruit and berry. Preserves included such exotics as green and yellow tomatoes, green apple, watermelon rind, and quince. There were ten or twelve kinds of pies, including some made from minced meat that I thought was moose but George said was elk.

The little fried pies were new to me. They were about a third the size of a conventional pie, and you could pick them up and eat them like a cookie. They were cooked in a special skillet that had several hollows about three inches across. The crust was shortening bread and the filling various kinds of preserves. The one I

Idaho

65

remember best was cherry. They were fried on open fires.

Cookies—at least a dozen kinds. My favorite had a soft center made of brown sugar and butter. There were chocolate cakes and fudge cakes and white cakes and yellow cakes and striped cakes and an upsidedown cake with watermelon-rind preserves substituting for pineapple. I gave that one a high mark. There was comb honey for the biscuits.

There were pickles of all kinds, from sweet to sour. The one I liked best was made from thin, crisp slices of turnip. George said he couldn't decide between the pickled onions and the green tomatoes. He also mentioned pickled eggs, but I don't remember them.

The plank tables were so jammed with dishes and bowls and trays of food that there was no room to put your platter. We sat on boards laid over sawhorses and on upended sections of logs and ate from plates in our laps. I ate until I was full to the tonsils, then walked around and shook it down and ate some more. I tried to sample some of everything, but that was an obvious impossibility compounded by the fact that I had inhaled a wild duck and half a blue grouse before pausing to catch my breath and make long-range eating plans.

A couple of the trout were next, then smoked salmon—that was delicious—then a lamb chop and some venison. I missed out on the deer liver, which George said was the best meat dish of all. Somewhere along the line I had some dark gravy that was rich with bits of something that tasted like burnt almonds. I don't think it was almonds, and I'm sorry I didn't find out for sure, because that was the tastiest gravy I ever experienced.

Then I started using the biscuits as a vehicle for comparing the jams, jellies, and preserves. They were big and crusty, and I could test three or four sweets with one of them. I tasted at least twenty of those goodies. A fried pie, some cookies, and a piece of

George Denny

cake, and I was through. It broke my heart to miss so many of those delicacies. The teeth and taste buds were willing, but the space was filled. I slid off the bench and went to sleep.

I awoke in about an hour as the sun dropped into the canyon downriver. The men were pitching horseshoes and polishing off the whiskey. The women were clearing the tables. Most of the guests would stay the night, and leftovers would be needed for another feast the next day.

After one taste of the whiskey, which was surely 110 proof and nearly choked me to death, I considered sampling another dessert or two. But it was no go—my enzymes were exhausted. Never before or since have I eaten as much as on that afternoon and no other food has ever tasted as good.

Open on Anything

Once there was a trout fisherman who remained calm and sensible in those critical days just before the opening of the trout season. I know that statement may be hard to credit, but it is true. His name was Ray Millholland, and he was a member of our trout-and-poker club, The Openers. That name was derived from the fact that we never missed an Opening Day, and also because our favorite poker game was Open on Anything.

Drawing strength and courage from some source denied the rest of us, Ray announced one spring that he would not open the trout season. He argued that he had gone up with us for three years, and not once had there been decent weather or fishing on the opening day. He vowed, therefore, that he would henceforth eschew the opening and wait for more friendly conditions when precious vacation time would not be wasted.

That was the year—I believe it was 1935—when The Day dawned warm and sunny and the water was clear and not too high. The first hatch—I remember they were small brown duns—began about ten in the morning, and from then on there were flies on the water all day. Trout rose to them greedily, and we all took limits of fine fish. Chick caught a sixteen-inch brook trout in the Sheep Ranch stretch of the Baldwin—the best *fontinalis* in the history of our club. Hank got into a nineteen-inch brown at the lower end of the Clay Hole and netted it one bend down, to win the pool for the biggest fish.

When we came home and told Ray about our good fortune he paled, uttered a corrosive oath, rushed out, and went on a three-day bender. He took up bird-watching and was not seen on a trout stream for nearly three weeks.

But his rational thinking deserved better fortune, for opening days do seem to provoke atrocious weather. Usually it rains, and streams are muddy and too high to wade comfortably.

As we drove home from these fiascos, cold, damp, and fishless, we would swear to be sensible next spring and wait for warm weather and clear water. That resolution would retain it's vigor the rest of the season and most of the following winter. Then, invariably, hope would dethrone reason. I remember one April that went approximately as follows:

Near the first of the month we had some warm, bright days and long-dormant angling hormones began to thaw and circulate. At such times The Openers hurry through lunch and congregate at the tackle shop like geese gathering for the northern migration. I retract that statement. Geese are highly intelligent, and they know when to go north.

For a few days we played it cool. We bought supplies, studied the new solunar tables, and relived last season's high lights. But as the good weather persisted, and as the big question was still unanswered, tensions mounted. Finally I could stand it no longer. I chirped, archly, that it wouldn't be long now.

All discussions stopped. Everybody looked at Chick. He was the oldest member, the cabin was always reserved in his

Open on Anything

69

name, and his word carried weight. He pursed his lips and gazed into space for long moments. Then he said, "Well, if this weather holds we certainly won't have to wait until June. Let's play it by ear and just be sure we don't tangle with snow or floods."

Everybody nodded happily. The defenses were crumbling. The last act of that sorry drama of wilting willpower might be called, "The Fly on the Windshield." It happened when I crossed the bridge on the way home from work. The large bug that spattered against the glass looked like a stone fly. I stopped at the end of the bridge and looked down. A fine hatch was hovering and dipping over the water.

There can be no more traumatic experience for a trout fisherman just before the opening. I hurried home and phoned Chick.

"A dandy hatch of big flies on the creek. They look like March Browns."

"I saw some on the canal not ten minutes ago," he said. "Come over this evening and we'll set things up. You bring Hank and I'll call the others. Bring your fly-tying kit."

I managed a fair degree of control at dinner, though the clear brown of the buillon was a poignant reminder of the color of the Baldwin as it emerges from the upper swamp. I skipped dessert and picked up Hank. Chick let us in and said, "I've reserved the big cabin for the opening. We've never given big streamers a fair chance. I mean really big ones. Do you have any number-six long shanks?"

Two days before the opening we met to make final plans. Ray was there; he never again made the mistake of being sensible. As usual, he put up a squawk about sleeping in the Army cot. He moaned that he had tossed fitfully in that sagging sack for years and demanded that we at least draw straws for the beds so he would have a chance to enjoy one trip. But he got nowhere with

George Denny

70

that beef, since beds were alloted on the basis of continued use and he had lost out when he missed the opening the time he was sensible. And no one felt sorry for him, because he was so generously upholstered he could probably sleep on a tick stuffed with restless porcupines.

At ten o'clock somebody switched on the radio for the news. The announcer said, "The weatherman warns that the cold front over Canada has turned south and will reach the northern part of the state tomorrow afternoon. Rain will be followed by snow, with freezing temperatures as far south as—"

Chick flicked off the radio and walked over and stared out the window. Nobody said a word. You could have heard a dry fly drop. At last he turned and said, "Hell and damnation. That stupid weatherman hasn't guessed right all winter. What do you say?"

By four o'clock the next day we were all in camp. We tossed our tackle on the beds and went to look at the river. It had been raining since noon, and the water was rising.

After supper we drew lots to see who fished where and with whom. Carol Klinger collected the money for our intricate series of pools—the most fish, the biggest fish, the biggest brown, the biggest brook, and so forth. Last-minute gut leaders were tied and put to soak in the washbasin. That was before nylon, and the washbasin was reserved for leaders. Any dude who wanted to wash or shave had to make other arrangements.

The spurts of cold rain now changed to snow. The situation was normal—all foul-weathered up.

So what? We were all in camp again after long, sterile months. We would give it a big try tomorrow, no matter what. The stove was hot, the laughter easy, the drinks and stories tall. Ray distributed the poker chips. Chick dealt the cards.

"Open on anything," he said.

Open on Anything

71

Arizona

Like any proper graduate, when I finished college in 1927 I felt I must see some of the world before settling down. A classmate, Bryce Gerard, heartily agreed. We bought a 1915 Ford from a farmer who lived two miles out of town. He assured us that he had driven it only once a week—to town and back on Saturday night. True or not, at fifty dollars that sturdy

little car with the square brass radiator was one of the best bargains of all time. It was a touring car with folding top and isinglass curtains. Somewhere in Kansas we encountered a wind-and-rain storm that blew the top off, but we didn't even stop for it. Didn't keep much rain out anyhow.

I couldn't have been more fortunate in my choice of companions. Bryce had been a scoutmaster and knew all the tricks for comfortable camping. This was important, since our families were not entirely happy with our plans and tried to discourage them by withholding any substantial financial backing. We would not be able to afford motels—cabins, they were called then. We would have to live pretty much on the country or find work if we expected to get far or stay long.

Bryce had a hanker to see Canada. I wanted to see the Rockies and the deserts. We flipped a coin, and I won. First the Southwest, winter there, then up the coast to Canada.

The trip took about two weeks. When the top of the car blew off, as mentioned earlier, we lashed ponchos over our gear in the back seat and kept rolling. An hour or so before sunset we would begin to look for side roads that would lead to a good camping spot. One rainy night a rancher let us take shelter in a shed recently used by pigs. We got used to the aroma in time, and in any case it was better than the storm outside. I remember one camp by a waterhole in the high desert—I think it was in New Mexico—when a herd of thirsty longhorns would have trampled us if we hadn't rolled under the Ford. Another hazard in that state was a washboard road that shook off one of the little kerosene carriage lamps and threatened much more serious damage until we reduced speed to a bumpy crawl. It took us all day to cover thirty or forty miles of that highway.

The dry desert air sucked moisture from the wooden spokes in the wheels until they were dangerously loose. We learned to shim them with little wedges and throw water on them at every opportunity. Otherwise the Ford behaved admirably, and we chugged into Phoenix with no further difficulties. Rain was falling there, the first time in nearly a year the natives told us, happily. They also assured us that work was hard to find anywhere near town and we would have a better chance up in the cow country. We gassed up with one of our few remaining dollars and headed north. In Prescott we heard that someone was building a dude ranch in the Verde Valley and might need help. So it was over the hump and down the long slope through Jerome and Clarkdale and past the copper smelters and through Cottonwood and out into the desert until we saw an unfinished building on a small mesa about fifty feet above the valley floor. That was the framework of

George Denny

74

what was to be named Rimrock Ranch. The boss man was sawing a timber. Could he find work for us? He could. Twenty dollars a month and board. Sold.

And so began our association with Romaine Loudermilk, who was known as "the Singing Cowboy." He knew all the usual western songs and some we had never heard. His "Blood on the Saddle" is still my favorite.

Romaine had another song I used to know in full. Now I've forgotten its name and several of the verses. What I can recall goes approximately as follows:

> Away up in the Mogollons (pronounced Mokiones)
> Among the mountain tops,
> A lion cleaned a yearlin's bones
> And licked his thankful chops,
>
> When who upon the scene should ride,
> A-trippin' down the slope,
> But High-chin Bob, of sinful pride
> And maverick-hungry rope.
>
> Well, glory be to me, says he,
> And fame's undying flowers,
> All meddlin' hands are far away,
> I ride my good top hoss today,
> And I'm top rope of the Lazy J,
> So kitty cat, you're ours.

Then there are a couple of verses about how he roped the cougar and tried to drag it to death.

Arizona

But ever as Bob turned and hoped
A limp remains to find,
A red-eyed lion, belly-roped
But healthy, loped behind.

Well glory be to me, says he,
This critter shore is tough,
But till the crack of judgment morn
I'll keep my dally round my horn,
For never any cowpoke born
Should stoop to holler " 'nuff."

The last couple of verses tell how Bob was not able to conquer that lion but never stopped trying. And legend holds that to this day the three are sometimes seen as ghostly apparitions up there in the Mogollons, Bob and his horse still trying to drag the lion to death.

Romie had been a partner in a dude ranch operation near Wickenberg. He reminisced approximately as follows:

"It was getting too crowded down there. We'd get a foreman broke in good, and some rich old gal would get hot for him and stake him to a spread of his own, and there'd be more competition. I sold out and came up here to find new country where my dudes can hunt and fish some."

As for the hunting and fishing, he chose well. There were plenty of desert quail and quite a few ducks. On a trip up the Blue Grade road toward Mormon Lake we saw a flock of a dozen or more wild turkeys. Romie was delighted to hear that. They had been nearly wiped out a few years earlier and the season was still closed, but the dudes would be glad to know they were coming back, he said.

There were thousands of antelope in the high country south

George Denny

76

and east of the valley; so many there would surely be an open season on them soon, he predicted. There were mountain lion under the Mogollon rim, and some of the dudes might like a chance at them. He asked Bryce and me to round up a pack of lion dogs, but that project failed for lack of suitable hounds.

As for fishing, there were bass in the Verde River near Cottonwood and trout farther up. The were plenty of trout in Oak Creek. We caught them on worms and grubs, and on one memorable afternoon we took at least thirty. None were larger than ten inches, and the hungry crew polished them all off that evening.

The desert quail were in flocks of one hundred or more; not the little coveys of bobwhite we used to see in Indiana. And those little speedsters ran us limp-legged through the mesquite and cactus before we found they were too fast for us. We learned to retreat a few steps as soon as we saw them, then swing out, come in from each side, and put the pinch on. This nearly always flushed a few, and the shots made others dive into cover and freeze. Those we could flush later. It was sporty shooting; they flew as fast and trickily as a bobwhite. But they weren't as good eating—a bit stringy and tasting of sage—though Lou, the cook, knew how to prepare them. He put them in the big spider with butter and bacon grease and seasonings, added a little water, put a lid on the spider, and smother cooked them low and slow. They came out tender and tasty.

Some mornings we would get up while it was still dark to try for the ducks as they came down from Montezuma's Well. Lou would have the big wood range roaring so it glowed red in spots, but the cook shack would still be bone-rattle cold. Lou would pour us mugs of coffee and pass the jug, and we would build up the coffee with dollops of the local corn whiskey. It was 1927, but those Verde Valley ranchers, like the ones in Idaho, had been

Arizona

77

making their own whiskey long before Prohibition and had seen no reason to stop. I remember that the Arizona whiskey was darker than the Idaho variety. Lou said it had been aged in oak for five years. He was a pale little man who had come to Arizona for his lungs. Whenever he coughed he took a slug of whiskey. He said it had kept him going for years.

Montezuma's Well was the largest body of water in miles, and ducks came from all over the valley to spend the night there. It was a couple of miles from the ranch, up Beaver Creek. Tens of thousands of years ago a huge spring had dissolved a great underground cavern in the limestone. Finally the roof fell in, and that made Montezuma's Well. There were pueblo ruins on its steep sides. The water was lukewarm, and the natives told us it was hundreds of feet deep. It flowed out through an orifice under the south rim and into an Indian irrigation ditch built along the creek. Romie said the ditch was more than a thousand years old, and its age could be proved by the thickness of the lime deposits on the banks. They built up at a rate of about one-half inch in a century and were more than six inches thick, he said.

At half-light we would clamber down the side of the mesa and hide in bushes on a ledge above the creek. The ducks came down right on the dot every morning, just before sunrise. Sometimes they were too high, but we usually managed to get a few fair chances. That was my first experience at what might be called pass shooting. Those birds were in a hurry. I burned a lot of powder before I learned to take enough lead. What finally taught me was a shot at a pair of pintails. I gave the first one what I thought was plenty of lead, and made a clean kill—on the second duck, which was at least twenty feet behind. After that I began to get my share.

I remember the breakfasts Lou whomped up for us. They were meant to power a man for a day's work. There were hot and

George Denny

78

cold cereals, milk, fruit juices, prunes, peaches, and apricots. There were the little fried pies I had first seen on the Gold ranch in Idaho. The big platter in the middle of the table held dozens of fried eggs, ringed with ham and bacon and sometimes sausages. Another platter was heaped with hash browns. Lou wouldn't fix both waffles and pancakes; we had one one day and the other the next. But there were always biscuits with either corn bread or corn muffins with plenty of butter, honey, maple syrup, and four or five kinds of jam and preserves. I almost forgot the pork chops. We had them or lamb chops every morning.

Lou refused to pick ducks, but he cleaned and cooked all the other game we brought him. We didn't bother the jackrabbits, but there were lots of little cottontails along the creek and in the irrigated fields. The men liked them and any other game we could contribute, and Romie gave us time off now and then to hunt and fish. It was much the same as I had found it in the Salmon River country; no limits, licenses, or seasons. Take what was needed and don't waste any.

Once when we were shingling the roof, a flock of about fifteen big Canada geese came honking up the valley and dropped into an alfalfa field a half mile away. Romie told us to try for them. Four of us made an elaborate stalk, approaching the field from all sides. Russell Boardman got one on the ground with a rifle. They came out over me but too high for the shotgun.

Boardman was a Bostonian who had known Romie at Wickenburg and was helping finance the new place. He was one of the few aviators of that day, and we had built a runway on the desert where he could land his Travelair biplane with one of the first Wright Whirlwind motors. A few years later he gained fame by flying nonstop for over five thousand miles, the longest such flight to that time. A year or so after that he died at Indianapolis in a takeoff accident in a cross-continent air race.

Arizona

Since the statute of limitations has surely run out I will admit to a crime that would be taken quite seriously today. It may have been illegal then, but if so we did not know it. We shot ducks at night, and I mean on the wing, not on the water or the ground. It was rare sport, and I've never heard of it before or since. And we didn't slaughter them as the duck clubs were doing in the day-time. The clubs were baiting ponds and using live decoys, and they murdered the ducks. We shot a few—a very few—at night by the light of the moon, and if you can think of a more sporting way, I will be glad to consider it.

Conditions had to be just right. The moon had to be within three or four days of full, either waxing or waning. And it could not be a perfectly clear sky, for then your only glimpse of a duck was a flick of the wing as it crossed the naked face of the moon. No one could get off a shot with that short a look. What was needed was a light cloud cover or haze that would silhouette the birds for several feet on either side of the moon; enough to get a line of flight and figure a lead.

Montezuma's Well was five or six hundred feet across, and it took several men to ring it right. We'd leave the horses a half mile away and slip up and take positions around the rim. Then we'd yell and throw rocks. It was about seventy feet down to the water, and in a few seconds the ducks would tower out. If you were lucky, some flew between you and the moon. After a shot we'd listen for a thump, then look for the down bird with a flashlight. Sometimes that desert moonlight was bright enough, even dulled by light clouds, so that a flashlight wasn't needed.

Sooner or later the ducks would return, since that was the only open water in miles, and we often got a second chance. But with five or six men we would seldom get that many birds. We disturbed their slumbers more than their numbers.

When we knew a bird was down and couldn't find it we

George Denny

80

would come back in the morning. Once I got there just as a coyote was finishing breakfast. He left me a lot of feathers and two yellow webbed feet.

Aside from Romie, the character I best remember at Rimrock was Digger, the Hopi Indian. He was our best stone mason. He lived about six miles down Beaver Creek, near Montezuma's Castle, and he walked it morning and evening. He looked about fifty but Romie said he wasn't more than thirty. He was stocky and strong. He would score a piece of sandstone with his trowel and break it over a scaffold upright like a piece of kindling. After he knew Bryce and me for a few weeks he apparently decided we were worthy and began to tell us all the best places to hunt and fish.

One story about Digger is worth telling. Some years ago I wrote it out and sent it to one of the slick magazines. I got it back with the following comment, ". . . the perfunctory pathos of the ending is out of one of fiction's stockrooms."

I doubt if that editor would believe me if I assured him the story is true. It is. I was there.

Everyone liked Digger but the foreman, Pinky. We called him that because he was an albino, with white hair and rabbit pink eyes. He was a hard worker and a fair boss in every way but that one. For some reason he disliked Indians. Maybe he was a hangover from those mountain men who used to say the only good Indian was a dead Indian. He rode Digger hard. He found fault with his work at every chance, but there weren't many of those, because Digger was a fine workman. Once Pinky jumped Digger for a mistake made by old Vance, the other mason. Digger stood on his scaffold and looked down at Pinky and took the abuse without a word. Finally, when Vance came over and straightened things out and took the blame, Digger smiled. Pinky whirled away, and I could see his teeth.

Arizona

Old Vance was a character, too. Romie said he was over ninety. He was six feet two or three and skinny as a stork. He had come from Texas years before; on account of a killing, the story went. He lived with his sister in a little 'dobe about a half mile from the ranch. She was older than he and nearly as tall.

Every morning Vance would shuffle up the road at about a quarter of eight and take a seat by the fire. For the next fifteen minutes, or until the foreman yelled, "frog," he would stuff the right side of his face with chewing tobacco. He would tamp it carefully into place with a bony forefinger, and when the job was done he would look like a lopsided gopher. The wad of tobacco would be nearly as large as a tennis ball.

Vance had no teeth and had to gum his chew. It lasted him all morning. When the foreman yelled, "straight up," at noon he would unfold down from the scaffold in lanky sections and scour the residue of the wad from his mouth with two or three dippers of water. Then he would eat the cherry pie his sister made each day for his lunch. Always cherry pie. After a short snooze he would yawn and stretch and begin to stuff his mouth with the wad of chewing that would last him until quitting.

In all the time I worked with Vance I never heard him say a word. Questions he couldn't answer with a nod or a shrug he would pretend not to hear. Romie said he could talk, but it was hard to understand him.

It was my job to keep the masons supplied. As they built the walls higher I rigged a hoist to lift them the mortar and rocks. We quarried the red sandstone slabs from an outcrop across the valley and trucked them up and spread them outside the walls. The two masons looked down from the scaffold to find the piece they needed next. They never spoke. Vance showed me the rock he wanted by splashing it with a squirt of tobacco juice. Digger

George Denny

indicated his choice by marking it with a dab of mortar flipped down from the point of his trowel.

One morning Digger was an hour late for work. He climbed to the scaffold, and I hoisted him the materials, and he began to prepare his mortar. Pinky strode over, put his hands on his hips, looked up at him and said, "When you think we start work here, Digger? You drunk last night?"

Digger didn't say a word, didn't look down, just kept troweling his mortar. Pinky began to rant at him.

"Damn you, Digger, when I ask you a question you by God answer," and on and on. I took the bucket and went for water. When I came back with it Digger was climbing down from the scaffold and Pinky was yelling at him to get back to work. Digger kept coming, and Pinky began to back away. He backed into an ell, and when he saw he was cornered he panicked. He pulled out his pocket knife and flicked out the blade. Digger picked up a length of two-by-four, and as he stooped for it Pinky got out of the corner and ran into his tent. I thought he would come out with a gun, and when he didn't I knew he was through on that job.

Romie had come around the corner just as Pinky pulled his knife. He asked me and a couple of others what had started it, and we couldn't tell him much. He walked over and looked up at Digger, who had climbed back to his scaffold, finished working his mortar, and was looking down at the slabs of sandstone.

"Damn it, Digger, I can't have a foreman who pulls a knife and runs from a fight but I won't have men who start fights, neither. You better have a good story or you're gone, too. What started it?"

Digger kept looking until he found the rock he wanted and splatted it with a dab of mortar. Then he turned his round, brown gaze on Romie.

Arizona

"Long time he give me bad talk, no reason. Today the same. He don't listen. He just yell. He call me no-good Indian sumbitch and I come down to fight him."

"What did you try to tell him? Why were you late?"

"My wife try to have baby last night. She try all night. Baby stuck inside. She die this morning. Baby die too."

Romie shook his head as though stunned and turned away. Then he came back.

"Jesus, Digger, that's a hell of a thing. I'm sorry. You take tomorrow off."

Digger nodded. I hoisted the rock to him. He buttered mortar and laid it in place. He tapped it twice with the handle of his trowel, stepped back, lined it up, and saw it was right. He looked down for another.

Trailer Life

The stock market fell on its face in late October of 1929. One month later I got married. She put up with my hunting, fishing, and other aberrations without serious complaint for more than forty-three years, and how could any man ask more?

For a few years during the Depression of the Thirties I was a reporter on the now defunct *Indianapolis Times*. Cubs were started at fifteen dollars a week. Since I played a fair game of golf and knew a birdie from a stymie, the city editor let me cover the local tournaments. Soon I was writing a daily golf column in addition to my work on the beats, and for that I was paid an extra three dollars a week.

Then I discovered that our State Conservation Department received reports from the wardens each Friday morning telling the condition of the water and the weekend fishing prospects in each district. This information they dispensed to any angler who cared to phone them. Why don't I run those reports in the Friday afternoon paper so you people won't have to answer so many phone calls? I asked. Why not, indeed? they agreed, and soon I was writing a daily outdoor column as well as the golf column and other duties, and that brought in another three dollars a week. Pretty good money in those days. People wanting to see their name in the paper invited me to hunt or fish on their property, and some of the spots were choice. I remember one little spring-fed pond on an estate not far from the city where the smallmouths were nearly always ready to take my hair frog or even a large dry fly. I say nearly because there were times when nothing would interest them, a truth well known to all bass fishermen.

I blame Ray Holland, long-time editor of *Field & Stream*, for our trailer trip. If he hadn't bought several fishing articles I doubt if the idea would have occurred to me. But those checks for forty, fifty, and once sixty-five dollars cast a spell. (I hasten to add that they pay a great deal more today.) That was a wonderful way to make a living—writing about the things you loved to do. But after I had covered the trout fishing in Michigan and the bass of Indiana, where could I find material for new articles? A trailer was the answer. A home on wheels. Free as a bird. Cover the continent. Follow the seasons. If you don't like where you are, move on.

I communicated all this enthusiasm to Ray Holland and suggested a monthly report on my adventures in a trailer. Their popularity was just beginning to burgeon, so he took me up on it. Twenty-five dollars a month.

Trailer Life

That did it. In a little shop in Terre Haute was a craftsman who had been making buggies and farm wagons for years. As that market waned he began to build house trailers; tiny things about ten feet long. Not enough room, said my wife, and we ended up with a twenty-footer, a monster in those days. Since we pulled it, the obvious name was 'Taffy."

The extra space was needed. We found a journalism student who was anxious to see the country and report her travels to her hometown newspaper, and she signed on as nursemaid at a stipend I am ashamed to report. But without Rosemary I could not have persuaded a reluctant wife to take the step. Our son was nearly four and our daughter a toddler of eighteen months, and they were not placid types. Help was required.

We left Indianapolis in February of 1936 during a thaw that followed one of the meanest cold spells the city had endured in many years. There was ice on the roads, and we crept along, often in second gear, until we found better traction south of Louisville. It took several days for me to get over the spooky feeling that I was being followed.

In northern Alabama the sun came out and we stopped shivering. My left elbow began to get a sunburn. Fairhope is, or was, a small town across the bay from Mobile. We parked in a pine grove near the beach, and the mayor came down to welcome us and arrange for an electrical hookup. Then we began to relax and enjoy trailer life.

The bunks were comfortable and the gasoline cooking stove adequate. Pine cones fueled the little heating stove on chill mornings. The children ate and played like small animals and began to tan. I fished every day for the largemouth bass and bluegills the natives called trout and brim. We picnicked on the beach and caught crabs with chunks of overripe meat tied to a string. The bay was cloudy from the winter runoff, and we

George Denny

couldn't see the crabs until we gently pulled them into shallow water where we could reach them with a net. Often they dropped the bait and backed away, but we always caught enough for a feast. We ate them boiled, with mayonnaise or butter sauce. I drool today at the memory.

One morning there was excitement at the Fairhope dock. A local fisherman had hooked a big sturgeon—eight feet long and too heavy to get in his boat. He towed it to the dock, and half the town came down to help him beach it. It was an ugly brute, but we were assured that its roe was worth a lot of money and the flesh even more.

When the commercial fishermen pulled in their nets of silver herring there were always a few odd specimens such as small red snappers or sea trout or even pompano. We bought these delicacies for literally pennies—the pompano cost fifteen cents—and had them in the pan before they stopped wiggling. Those fish, some free and the rest cheap, were a great help to a tight budget. We had allotted two dollars a day for food for the five of us, and we ate well for that or less.

After two weeks we moved on. My most vivid memory of Florida is the evening we spent at Tarpon Springs. The Greek sponge fishermen docked their boats there, and it happened to be the day before the fleet put out to sea. Captains were buying drinks for their crews, and we sat in a dim corner of the tavern and watched the celebration. We saw a crippled man carried to his chair by his shipmates. We learned he had been stricken by the bends, that scourge of divers, some years before. But he continued to dive because it was only at twenty or thirty fathoms, encased in steel and rubber, that the pressure somehow overcame his paralysis. On the bottom of the ocean he was a whole and useful man again and gathered as many sponges as any diver on his ship.

Trailer Life

The men sang songs in Greek, accompanied by a zitherlike instrument one of them held on his lap. After an obviously sad rendition my wife asked one of the men what it was about. In broken English he replied that it was a very old song about a hero coming home from many adventures. He forgot to change his sail from black to white as he came into the harbor, and his father thought his son had died and threw himself into the sea and was drowned.

My wife and I looked at each other.

"Theseus?" she whispered.

I nodded. We were listening to Homeric legends sung by descendants of Ulysses.

We were on the road six months before I reluctantly admitted I would not be able to make a decent living for my family by gypsying around in a trailer and writing about it. But the determining factor was that my wife was then two months pregnant, and patient and permissive as she was I could hardly expect her to find room in the trailer for a crib.

We had hoped to see the Pacific and even some of Canada, but got only as far west as Sante Fe, New Mexico. The trout fishing there will be covered in another chapter. On the way home we stopped for a couple of weeks at Boulder, Colorado. There, in addition to Boulder Creek, I fished a tiny lake high in Estes Park where trout rose only once each day, shortly after noon, and then only for about ten minutes. That, too, is another story.

And so, in July of one of the hottest, dustiest summers in many a year, we crossed the Dust Bowl on our return to Indianapolis. Rosemary and the two children rode in the trailer; it was legal then. Temperatures were often over a hundred, and the dry winds were laden with topsoil. The children were naked as baby birds most of the time, and Rosemary draped them with wet towels and fashioned moist cotton masks for them to breathe through when the dust was heavy. And it was brutal; often we could not see a quarter of a mile at noon.

So ended our adventures in a trailer. I loved it, the children were not harmed by it, and my wife was at least kind enough, I thought, not to complain about it, which shows that men have no business trying to second-guess women. In writing this I turned to her to verify some memory that was hazy after thirty-five years. She set me straight, then cupped her chin in her hands and sighed.

"It was fun, wasn't it, even with the responsibility of the children. Without them it would be a ball. Let's get one of those fancy aluminum models and try it again."

And do you know, I think she meant it.

Trailer Life

Chick's Chicken

Noteworthy in the annals of our trout-fishing club, The Openers, is the story of the night Chick brought home the wrong chicken. It took months to learn the truth. At first all we knew for sure was (1) that Chick had somehow provoked a serious domestic crisis, (2) because of which he might not be able to come up with us for the opening of the trout season, and that (3) Mrs. Chick wore a lovely new caracul jacket to church on Easter, and (4) at that service the minister announced a generous gift to the missionary fund from an anonymous donor, meanwhile gazing benignly at Chick, who had a bandage under his left eye.

Since Chick did get up for the opening that spring we deduced that (3) and (4) were penance done for (1). But details of his transgression and the reason for the bandage were unknown. At first Chick refused to talk, but finally all the guesses and gossip were distilled into a scandalous story by Mrs. Probe, our most voluble tattle, and Chick saw he must clear the air.

"I hoped the whole stupid business could just blow over and be forgotton," he sighed. "Any explanation I try to make is bound to bring up that hassle with Ray last fall. Remember the last afternoon of the season when I fished the Sheep Ranch stretch of the Baldwin by mistake?"

I nodded. Mistake or not, Chick had been guilty of a grievous error. One does not, under threat of excommunication, fish water assigned to another club member. And the fact that Chick got into a seventeen-inch brown and Ray came around the bend just in time to see him land it—well, that was hard to forgive and forget. To compound the trouble, the fish won the pool for the largest taken that month. Chick offered the prize money to Ray, who refused it haughtily, and there were words.

"I didn't want to stir all that up again," Chick continued. "If I had read the assignments right on that last trip this other stupidity wouldn't have happened. All in all, it makes me look like nine kinds of a knothead."

His story, with many a halt and digression, took some time to tell. Briefly it was follows:

On that fateful evening Mrs. Chick phoned just as he was about to leave the office. She said the minister and his wife had dropped in for tea, had made no move to leave, and had accepted her invitation to dinner. With only leftovers in the icebox better fare would have to be found, and quickly. Would Chick pick up a couple of small fryers, dismembered and ready for the pan, and come home right away, please, dear. And, oh, yes, a head of lettuce.

And now a word of explanation for you youngsters. This all took place back in the early Thirties, before supermarkets and cellophane. In those days when domestic fowls were needed for the table we usually went to the downtown market and made a choice from the pens of live birds. It was well to pause outside

Chick's Chicken

the door leading to that noisome section, take a deep breath, dash in and make a selection as rapidly as possible. Then we did other errands while the bird was plucked and cleaned.

It was about ten days before the opening of the trout season. For weeks Chick, like all proper anglers, had been repairing tackle, tying new batches of flies, and thinking of little but that happy day. He had planned to drop in on Joe after dinner to wangle some hackle for making Ginger Quills, the only fly pattern needed to arm him properly for the opening. As he walked into the market area where the chickens were penned he realized that project would have to be put off to another day, with time running short.

There was a far corner of the poultry section where culls were penned, usually tough, old roosters good only for soup. Once in a blue moon one of those rejects had usable hackle feathers, and Chick always examined them carefully. This time the moon was blue. Crouched in the end pen was a long-legged, wry-necked game cock. He looked promising. Chick stuck a finger through the wire, and the bird raised his hackles and took a savage swipe at it. No doubt about it; those neck feathers were a perfect shade of light honey with the rare, dark centers; an exciting find.

Ordinarily Chick would have beckoned the clerk over and bargained him down to about fifty cents, since he would have no idea about some of the finer things of life, such as hackle feathers. But at that moment disaster loomed. The door opened and in walked Ray, heading straight for the cull corner. He, too, was a fly tier.

Under normal conditions Chick would have welcomed him with a fraternal cry and after some banter and haggling offered to share the prize. But with relations still strained by the misunderstanding of the previous season he feared that Ray would

George Denny

have no mercy. In that case and with such a prize at stake, bidding might reach record heights.

Chick hesitated not one moment. He opened the pen, subdued the rooster after a spirited flurry, dashed to the cashier's stand, grabbed a length of string, tied the legs together, tossed the puzzled clerk a bill, and fled.

And now let us pause a moment and consider why Chick, a model husband, a pillar of the church, a sensible and successful citizen, should so forget himself. The answer, of course, is Fishwish, that aberration that afflicts all dedicated trout fishermen in the sensitive days just before the opening of their angling season. Fishwish is discussed at length in the next chapter.

Chick drove home in a happy daze and parked in his driveway. As he stepped from his car, rooster in hand, he slipped in a patch of slush and fell heavily into a puddle. It was then, as they both sprawled on the ground, that the rooster got in a vicious peck under Chick's left eye. Undaunted, he arose, marched into the house dripping mud and blood, raised the bird aloft, and exulted—"Hot diggety damn, honey, look what daddy found."

Then he saw the guests and remembered the fryers. And the lettuce.

That's exactly what happened. There's not a word of truth in Mrs. Probe's report that Chick came home falling-down drunk and cursed the minister and his wife.

The Dread Fishwish

The following is fiction only to the extent that I have taken a series of happenings and rearranged them to make a coherent report. Every incident in it actually occurred; if not to me to one of my trout fishing companions. Dr. Dendrite is not a Ph.D., and his and other names have been changed to protect the guilty.

My friend and fishing companion, Henderson Dendrite, Ph.D., soon will publish a study of the mental stresses that beset trout fishermen prior to the opening of the fishing season each spring. He has named the condition Fishwish.

"It's a functional nervous disorder; a psychoneurosis related to hysteria," he explained. "Psychosis is too strong a term, although it may seem a valid description in some aggravated cases. Very little work has been done on it. About thirty years ago a Canadian psychologist described a few typical cases. He called it Anglemania. I think Fishwish is a better term. More descriptive."

"Put it in layman's language, Doc," I said. "Remember, I'm a correspondence-school dropout."

"The cause is obvious. The victim wants to fish and can't because the season is closed. Pressure builds during the long winter months. The frustration is cumulative and peaks out just before the opening of the season. Strange things happen in those critical days. Solid, dependable citizens who are devoted husbands and loving fathers become vagrant and irresponsible. The worst of it is that they are not aware of their condition and can't or won't see how they are afflicted. Take you, for example. Of course you are a bit more disordered than the average."

"I never felt better," I said.

"Naturally. The season is two weeks old and you have been up to the camp twice. The first day on the stream is a sure cure. But I wish you had been able to stand off and take a clear look at yourself a month ago. You were no worse than usual for that time of year but it wasn't a happy sight."

"Let's have it," I said.

"My notes on you are right here. Your good wife, Helen, has been giving me complete reports on your pre-trout-season activities for the past three years. But before I say another word, promise you will hold none of this against her. She did it in the interest of science and because of our long friendship. She may also have had some faint hope for a cure."

"Cross my heart," I said.

"Good," he said, shuffling his notes. "This year you began to get that vacant, glazed look about the third week in March, roughly six weeks before the season opened. On March twenty-ninth you refused to go to a PTA meeting."

"PTA, schmeeTA," I said. "She doesn't expect me to go to all those meetings with her."

"That was the meeting when she was inducted as vice-president and as an added attraction the mayor was to announce that your son had won the scholarship. But you had promised Henry you would pop over that evening and show him how to salvage a tacky fly line and of course you couldn't disappoint an old fishing buddy."

"You're kidding—when—who," I fumbled.

"March twenty-ninth, as I just said, and the facts are exactly as stated. Then a few days later there was the matter of the feathers you pillaged from Helen's new Easter hat. She reports that you explained, with a perfectly straight face, that they were a rare shade you had been seeking all winter and that you needed them to fashion—" He paused and studied his notes. "It says here 'some Redwing Coachman flies.' "

"Leadwing Coachman," I corrected, with dignity. "I remember the incident perfectly. I told her to buy another hat, the best in town."

"Ah, yes, but that was when she discovered the crime, just before church on Easter morning," Doc continued, mercilessly. "Then on April nineteenth, you came home early for some sad reason and found Edna in your den. Helen says that paragon of cleaning women will never set foot in your house again."

"But, Doc, listen," I protested. "I'd been sorting flies and had them laid out all over the table and bench. That—that witch came in and flung open all the windows. There were dry flies everywhere. I finally found Hewitt's Neversink Skater, but some of the little size eighteens and twenties are still missing."

"That does shed new light on the matter and I will amend my notes to show a degree of provocation," said Doc, busily amending. "But the facts remain that your neighbors are still talking in awed tones about the profane hell you raised, Edna is lost, and Helen is sad about it. I could go back to last spring and the one before that and catalogue more of your sins, but I'm sure you get

The Dread Fishwish

99

the picture. The point is that you are just one of many. My studies show that Fishwish troubles all proper trout fishermen to some extent."

He tamped a load into his pipe and lighted it.

"I know of one case where Fishwish nearly caused a divorce. The couple were married just before Christmas after a short courtship and she had no idea of his passion for trout fishing. She was at first puzzled and then a bit disturbed as he lapsed into his spring aberration, but managed to put up with him until a couple of days before the opening. Then he flipped.

"He was tying some bucktails and ran out of both deer hair and squirrel tail. While casting about in a Fishwish frenzy for some substitute he recalled the luxuriant ruff on his wife's prize Pekingese. It wouldn't have been so bad if the pooch hadn't been entered in an important bench show the following week. So, when he came back from the opening trip his bride had gone home to mother and her lawyers served him with papers. Fortunately, the preliminary hearing was before old Judge Ramsey and you remember what a devoted trout fisherman he was. He knew what happens to anglers in those sensitive times and he understood what caused the rape of the Peke's ruff. He was able to smooth things over and save the marriage, but it was a damned close thing."

"Now wait a minute, Doc," I said. "You are just as rabid a trout fisherman as any of us. How can you be objective about this?"

"A fair question," he admitted. "I used to be as touched as any of you. But have you forgotten that for the last three winters I have flown down to Argentina for a couple of weeks of that wonderful fishing? That relieves all my Fishwish tensions. Then I can come back here and observe the twitchings and gibberings of you and your ilk with clinical detachment."

George Denny

"You mean cynical amusement," I accused.

"No, no," he protested. "It is not amusing. There are millions of trout fishermen and nearly all are afflicted to some degree. There's grave potential for trouble there, up to and including broken homes. Wives and relatives must be taught what to expect and why, and comforted with assurance that the first fishing trip of the season will cure the most alarming case. Much patience and understanding are necessary."

He refreshed our drinks and reactivated his pipe. After a few puffs he leaned back in his chair and smiled.

"How do I know this study is important and why did I undertake it?" he asked. "Who do you think ruined that Peke's ruff?"

Morels

To this day I can't understand why it took me so long to discover morel mushrooms. Discover is not the right word. I had seen them many times and dismissed them as a strange-looking fungus that was probably dangerous. I knew and appreciated puffballs and the little button mushrooms with pink gills that grew on our golf courses. That was the extent of my interest in mycology.

Louis Bromfield, an acknowledged gourmet, had this to say of morels: "I place them at the very top of all delicacies, far above *pate de foie gras* and salmon trout and *ecrivisse*, far above the ordinary mushroom—"

I was thirty-five when I learned what I had been missing. I remember thinking that based on the Biblical three score and ten years, half my life had been wasted as far as morels were concerned. And that, my friends, was a grievous waste indeed. Youngsters, do not let it happen to you. And as for you oldsters who have not yet tasted them, all you can do is try to make up for the lost time.

With very few exceptions morels occur only in the spring. I hear there are rare times when a few are found in the fall, but I have never seen one then. It takes a certain amalgam of warmth and moisture to bring them forth. If a spring is cold and wet, they will not appear until the sun has warmed the ground for several days. On the other hand, if the ground is warm and dry, they will pop up in hours after a good rain. In central Indiana this combination of circumstances usually occurred in late April, so that must have been the time when I fished Cornstalk Creek with Carol Klinger in the spring of 1940.

There had been showers the day before, and Carol feared the water might be too roily. If so, we would hunt morels, he said. They were due any moment. The May-apple was beginning to bloom, and that was sure sign.

But the water was perfect, and I rigged up with a small streamer behind a brass spinner. Carol fished a hair frog. The stream wasn't large enough for two abreast, so we took turns, a pool at a time. About an hour later we had a couple of keeper smallmouths apiece. Carol was on the bank watching me fish my stretch when he suddenly yelled, "Morels, morels."

I worked on up through the pool and took one more keeper, then went back to where Carol was still ranging in circles. He had taken the fish out of his creel, and it was half full of those funny-looking fungi.

"Is that what they are?" I asked. "They look dangerous. I wouldn't eat one for much money."

"That's fine," he said. "All the more for me."

We fished no more that afternoon. We filled his creel and then mine and then filled our hats. The strange little mushrooms were scattered throughout that meadow, and there were a few in a woodlot that adjoined it. They looked like a sponge on a

Morels

stalk. Some were no larger than my thumb; some three or four inches tall. Some were nearly round, some egg-shaped, some long and thin. Some were light yellow, some shaded into brown. But all had the pitted, spongelike texture that distinguishes the several species and makes it impossible to mistake them. Not one of the five true morels is dangerous. All but one are rated delicious. There are three false morels, and they differ so from the true ones there is no chance for trouble.

Morels can be found throughout the United States, except in arid or subtropical regions. I have found them in the San Gabriel mountains at an altitude of about three thousand feet, early in March. My son found them in the high Sierras at about ten thousand feet, late in the summer. The snow had just melted there, so it was the equivalent of early March lower down. But I think they are best known and appreciated through the mid-west and in the northern tier of states. I hear there are places in northern Michigan where they can be harvested by the bushel, and I would like to see that crop and be able, just once, to have my fill of morels.

That evening at Carol's house I cleaned the bass while he split and washed the morels. He got out his largest skillet, spread it liberally with butter, and heaped it with morels. He cooked them slowly, and they simmered down into a spongy cake. Carol's wife was the third for dinner, and Carol cut the cake into three equal parts.

"Not for me," I said. "I'll fry this bass."

"Don't be ridiculous," he said. "Put the bass in the icebox. One bite of this and you'll forget fish."

He was right. I had never tasted anything quite so good. I will not try to describe it. It must be experienced. Carol cooked a second lot and then a third, and we could have handled more. Morels are mostly water, and they simmer down to a fifth of their original size, or even less, when sautéed in butter. That's

George Denny

the way to cook them, and don't talk to me about using them to garnish a steak. No steak I've ever eaten could add to the flavor of morels.

That's all I'm going to tell you. Maybe I've said too much already. Next spring if I catch you picking morels at any of my favorite spots, I'll rue the day I wrote this.

I have written inserts and additions to several of these chapters but none have given me the pleasure I find in this effort. Only a few paragraphs back I said I had heard there were places in northern Michigan where morels could be harvested by the bushel. I know now that is close to the truth. Quarts, certainly, even now and then a peck or more. As I write this I am full to the gills with fresh morels. I have stuffed myself with them for several days. I have literally, for the moment at least, had my fill.

And they were just as delicious as I remember them that night at Carol Klinger's house nearly thirty-five years ago. Best of all, we just had a cold spell before the season was really well along and the natives assure us that the best is yet to come. And I'll be ready for more in a day or two, or as soon as the sun warms the moist ground again.

Places where morels and woodcock can be found are much the same in one respect. Those fortunates who know where they are will not tell a stranger. A close friend or relative, perhaps. When we first came here, to a resort near Traverse City, and heard that the first morels were beginning to pop, we begged and we pleaded. The replies were vague. "Oh, you're apt to find them anywhere," was the usual answer. But we were lucky. We found a man who was deeply indebted to us and he showed us a wood where they were thick.

Eureka!

Morels

Woodcock

Indiana has never been noted for its woodcock hunting. Rarely, very rarely, we might see one when out after quail, ducks, or rabbits. Once Father came home from a hunt in the northern part of the state with three of the little timberdoodles. He reported that he and his companion had stumbled into a lot of them in a big stand of willows. There were at least thirty of them in an acre or two. Flight birds on the way south from Michigan or Canada, we decided.

It was Bill Sully who told me about the Valley of the Anawak. Where he learned of it I do not know and did not ask. Charley Cox once wrote an article about it, and it may be Sully wormed the location out of him. He swore me to secrecy, of course. That is standard practice. I will cheerfully go your note or lend you my Leonard rod or trust you with my wife, but if I know good woodcock cover I would not betray it to you unless satisfied you would not talk if subjected to the Chinese water torture.

I promised, and Sully took me there. The valley was about forty-five miles from Indianapolis. It was less then a mile long. A tiny, spring-fed brook crept through its lush willow thickets. There were nearly always woodcock there. Native birds nested on nearby slopes and came down to probe for worms in the rich, black soil of the thickets. In the fall the flight birds stopped for a rest and a meal, and at times there were hundreds there. I know that sounds like an improbable claim, but I have seen such concentrations more than once.

I was never sure of the spelling of Anawak or from whence the name derived. Years later I read in a Stanton Delaplane column, "It turns chilly up here in Mexico City, 7400 feet high in the Valley of Anahuac."

Indiana men fought in the Mexican War and brought back names for two towns—Vera Cruz and Montezuma. Maybe that's where they got the name for that woodcock cover. It's certainly a sound-alike.

My wide-open twenty double was perfect for woodcock. In those willow thickets you had to get off your shot at fifteen yards, or less. I think one reason Sully took me there was that I was a snapshooter. He used me to beat out the heaviest parts of the cover, knowing I liked the close shooting. He worked the edges and took the birds I missed or didn't see. We made a good team.

Anawak was beautifully hidden. No road came near it except at the lower end. There was a farm house, but in all the years I hunted there I never saw the place.

John Alden Knight, an authority on woodcock, wrote that they were so undependable one could never be sure to find them in a given place at a given time. The Valley of the Anawak belied

Woodcock

that statement. In fourteen years I went there at least thirty times. Not once did I fail to find woodcock, though there were days when they were flushing wild and flying fast and trickily. More than once I failed to get the limit.

But the point is that there were always some there, except possibly in the dead of winter, and considering Knight's statement, it may be that the Valley of the Anawak was the finest, the most dependable woodcock cover in the entire United States. And it was only an hour from my home.

Woodcock are unpredictable. Some waft gently up in easy range and fly away in the open. But it's well to expect the worst—a sneaky rise and a fast and twisty flight that takes advantage of all possible cover. Some twitter as they get up, some are quiet as ghosts. I've seen them fly away, barely skimming the ground, through the densest thickets. I've had them flush at my feet and

George Denny

dodge back over my head. But the usual rise is straight up and out through the top of the willows. If you don't get them before they top out, that's probably the last you'll see of them. Actually, three men are better than two in beating out a willow thicket. The one working the middle should get a few snap shots, but the ones on either side may have better chances.

I began to look for other woodcock cover and found a few places. Nothing to remotely compare with Anawak but worth a try after a storm that might bring flight birds. Without exception, these were willow thickets with the black, moist soil rich with worms. I also learned to look for the droppings, fresh white splashes that were a sure sign.

I remember one spot along a tiny rill that flowed into Sugar Creek. One day a business errand with my wife took us within a few miles of the place. I had given no thought to hunting as we left home that morning, but there happened to be a shotgun and a few shells in the car trunk. She agreed to help me beat the cover after I assured her it wasn't too thick and the ground wouldn't be muddy.

She followed me through an opening in the brush that bordered the willows and we had no sooner stepped into the dim thicket than two birds got up. I got the first as it towered. The second one whirled around behind me, right over her head. I yelled "Drop," and she did. I shot over her to get the second bird as she sprawled on the ground. Then I had sense enough to help her up and brush her off and praise her loudly for the her quick thinking. She took the brace back to the car and waited until I found and downed two more singles. That didn't take ten minutes, but she never let me forget it.

The only dog we used to hunt the Anawak willows was our old Ruby. That bitch was a character. Father got her in some kind of a trade when she was about six years old. She was too slow for

Woodcock

the doctor who owned her. He wanted a dog that would get out and cover a forty acre field in a couple of passes. Not Father. He'd had too many wild ones that flushed birds and chased them out of sight while he whistled himself blue in the face. He wanted a dog that was steady and sure, even if slow. Ruby was that dog. I'll have more to say about her in a later chapter.

When we first tried Ruby in the Anawak willows she wasn't much interested. We'll find no quail in those thickets, she indicated. She insisted on hunting the open stretches. Finally I kicked out a woodcock and dropped it in front of her. I asked her to fetch, but she wouldn't. She nosed it and then looked at me as though to ask if that was what we were after. I assured her that it was. I picked the bird up and stroked its feathers and let her nose it again. From that moment she pointed woodcock for us. She made it plain that she preferred quail and was doing it only because we seemed to need her help. She didn't like the heavy cover and skirted it when possible. But if there were woodcock there she went in and pointed them. She wouldn't retrieve but always found the downed birds and stayed with them until we picked them up.

One spring I went to the Valley of the Anawak to hunt morels. On the way down the long slope that led to the floor of the valley a woodcock flushed a few feet ahead. I knew there must be a nest and began to look for it. A cautious inch at a time I crept forward toward the spot where the bird had jumped. It was largely luck that I found that nest. The four speckled eggs were covered with two dead leaves. At a certain angle I could look under the curled edge of one leaf and see them. Then I knew what I had long suspected; the valley had native birds.

Years later I read how ruffed grouse will hide their eggs with dead leaves when they leave the nest. The author said the mother bird would position two leaves, one on either side of the nest, so

George Denny

110

that when she flushed at the approach of danger the leaves would fall inward and hide the eggs. I believe that's exactly what that woodcock did.

Now that the Valley of the Anawak is ruined, perhaps Sully will forgive me if I admit breaking my promise. I took a stranger hunting there. Henry Weed, a business associate, was born and raised in Savannah, Georgia, and a mighty hunter was he. His family had owned a plantation, a city house, and Ossabaw Island. The latter was some ten thousand acres of wilderness just off the coast, and it was rich with every game bird and animal known to that country. Henry's father was hardware distributor for the area, and the Weeds shot only Parker shotguns.

One of his hunting stories is worth repeating if only to remind us of the good old days. Hank's father took one of the gun salesmen hunting, and on the way to the blinds they made a wager on who could get the most birds with one box of shells. The limit was twenty-five in those days. Gun salesmen had to be expert shots to properly promote their products, but Hank's father was willing to try the man. Both men dropped their birds until each had twenty-three down. Hank's father missed with his twenty-fourth shell. The salesman went on to complete his string. Hank's father waited until two birds crossed and got them both with his last shell. A standoff.

In one of his reminiscences Hank used a term I had never heard. He referred to their "river nigger" and in answer to my question it developed he was a servant who spent all his time gathering seafood for the family and the other blacks. I will risk the displeasure of the black community in using that term, for it seems important to tell of that vanishing breed of bizarre characters who were hand-me-downs from the days of slavery. Hank said many southern landowners had river niggers in those days—the first quarter of the century. Since I hadn't seen him in

Woodcock

many years, I wrote to confirm my memories. His reply, in part, follows:

"You ask about our river nigger. His job was to see that we had at least two kinds of fresh seafood; shrimp, fish, crabs or oysters *every day* while we summered on the salt water estuary. Our life for those months was a delight. There were great expanses of salt marsh—most prolific. We lived in a rambling frame house on a high bluff, surrounded by live oaks, camelias, azaleas, etc.

"Our river nigger was named Book John. He was half bald because he fell in a crab pot when he was a pickanniny and scalded his scalp. He was slight; about 150 pounds, but a master of a bateau—could row for hours. He was an artist with the cast net—could spread a ten foot diameter net perfectly with a graceful, swinging motion—and he knew every fishing drop in the area.

"He took to the river whenever the tide was right and I often accompanied him on those trips as did my brothers and my sister. A typical day's catch was a bushel of shrimp and ten dozen crabs, all of which were cooked outside in a big, cast-iron pot, the kind missionaries are boiled in."

Hank bragged a bit about his hunts in Georgia, and our Indiana sport suffered by comparison. Once he told of a banner day—a limit of ducks, a limit of quail, a wild turkey, and best of all, two woodcock. Those last were rare and valued birds, he said, and it was a great day when he got even one. My Hoosier pride could take no more.

"Hank," I said, "how would you like to get a limit of woodcock in an hour or two tomorrow morning?"

He looked at me and smiled unbelievingly.

"Jawidge," he said with his delightful accent. "You're funnin' me."

"I'll pick you up at eight," I said. "We'll be home for lunch.

George Denny

112

But I'm breaking a solemn promise by taking you there, and I'll have to blindfold you for the last few miles. You understand why that's necessary, of course?"

"Certainly," Hank agreed without a moment's hesitation.

Blindfold him I did before we turned off the main highway and onto the side roads that led to the hallowed spot. And the Valley of the Anawak did not fail me. Some flight birds were down, and we each had a limit of four in less than an hour. Best of all, neither of us missed a shot, although it took old Ruby to keep the slate clean. Hank's last shot was a desperate snap as the bird dived behind a screen of leaves. We searched for several minutes before Ruby ranged out a few yards and found the cripple. As usual she would not pick it up; just stood looking at it until we got there.

The Valley of the Anawak is no more. That beautiful spot, possibly the finest woodcock cover in the entire country, was destroyed by one of the damned dams of the damn Army Corps of Engineers. There were a dozen other places where they could have put that dam; places where there would have been as much or more fishing and swimming and boating for as many or more people. But, no, they had to put it in the one place where it ruined that unique, that wonderful cover. May they languish forever in Hades, splashed by the white droppings from great flocks of woodcock that circle over them endlessly.

Grouse

There's no use putting it off any longer. Sooner or later I will have to tell about my one hunt for ruffed grouse, and it might as well be now.

Business required that I move from Indiana to the West Coast in 1949. Up to that time, in more than thirty years of hunting, fishing, and just plain prospecting, I saw only two wild grouse in Indiana. Since then their numbers have increased to the point where there is an open season and some fair-to-middling shooting there now.

Not so when I lived there. They were scarce and protected. Hoosier hunters who wanted grouse went to Michigan or Wisconsin. They brought back many a tale of the wariness of the gray ghost, and not many birds. They all agreed it was the toughest wild fowling they had ever known. You have to shoot at the noise of their rise—shoot where you think they will be —you don't get a decent look at one in ten—so went their complaints.

All of which only whetted my desire to it. I rated myself a better-than-average wing shot with emphasis on snap shooting in heavy cover. If the sad truth must be known, I even bragged a little about what I would do to grouse when given a chance.

That chance came one fall on a trip to the Baldwin area of central Michigan with Bill Sully and Ad Howe. We hunted the swamps and swales for two days. There were plenty of birds. I fired twenty-three shells.

It was as advertised. I didn't see many of those birds. I shot at the noise of their rise. I shot through brush where they might be. I didn't get one.

Two or three of those grouse were in sight and range long enough for me to score. I should have brought back at least one. Maybe two. I didn't. Neither did Ad Howe. Sully got one.

The sting of that defeat—better it be called humiliation in view of my brags—is still with me, but over the years it has mellowed from shame to respect. I want another chance at ruffed grouse. I'll be shooting the same little twenty double, and maybe I'm a mite surer with it now. But this time there will be no advance boasting about what I'm about to do to those so-and-sos.

My wife's family had a summer cottage at Northport Point, on Grand Traverse Bay in northern Michigan. One spring we went up ahead of the season to prepare it for renters. There was a path through the woods and out to the rocky point, and as we walked it one morning a grouse fluttered out of the brush and down the path ahead of us, dragging a wing and trying to indicate that she couldn't possibly make it much farther. I'd seen that performance more than once while trout fishing in the spring but never with a companion. This time I knew what to do. I told my wife to follow the mother bird until she recovered and disappeared and then sit down and wait for me to call.

Grouse

While she followed the seeming cripple down the path I withdrew a few steps and hid in thick bushes about thirty feet from where the grouse had emerged. In about five minutes she came slipping back along the path, pausing now and then to look and listen. She went to the place we had first seen her and stepped onto a little hummock. For long minutes she stood there, unmoving. Then I saw her beak open in an utterance I couldn't hear. Instantly she was surrounded by tiny bits of birds no larger than my thumb. She stepped down to the path and started to lead them away.

When I emerged from my cover she uttered another command and the babies disappeared. But now I knew exactly where to look. Ignoring mama's frantic flutterings I approached the spot where I had last seen the tinies. When I got to within a few feet I dropped to my hands and knees and proceeded an inch at a time, turning over leaves and probing every bit of cover. Finally I found them. They weren't under leaves or in grass; they had simply squatted down and closed their bright little eyes the instant mama spoke the word. Some were on dead leaves, some on bare ground. It made no difference; they faded perfectly into any background. I called my wife, and we admired them for a few moments before allowing the mother to decoy us away again.

I'd like to shoot a ruffed grouse or two if only to regain some feeling of competence. But if I don't, if I never again look at one over the barrels of the twenty, nothing can take from me the picture of those tiny birds by the woods path, and I wouldn't trade that memory for several limits.

P. S. I finally did it. Got my grouse this fall. Heard about forty, saw seven or eight and got four. The little 20 improves with age.

George Denny

116

The Springhouse

Now I understand why Father seemed so beglamoured with life on a farm. He never owned or worked on one but was forever driving about the countryside, cozying up to farmers. He had a sound reason for this. He was making friends with and influencing people who had a covey or two of quail or a stretch of good bass water on their land. As a happy consequence we never lacked places to hunt and fish.

It must have been on one of those scouting trips that he discovered the opening on the threshing crew and arranged for me to fill it. It was a hot, dry July, and if you have ever toiled on a threshing crew, you will know what I mean when I say, plaintively, that it was asking a lot of a city boy of thirteen. We were at war with Germany, and Father pulled out all the patriotic stops—boys had to fill in for the fighting men, et cetera. I did my best for about ten days, and then the heat, dust, and long hours overcame my pride, and I begged off. Father was not pleased with me but did his best to hide it.

Memories of those strenuous days are hazy now. I drove a long flatbed wagon. A man walked on either side and forked sheaves of wheat onto it. When it was heaped high I drove to the threshing machine, a stream-driven monster that devoured the bundles as fast as we could feed them to it. We worked long hours, and there were no coffee breaks. We paused only when the water boy came by, then we took two dippers. The first we drank, the second we poured over our dusty heads. There was an air of urgency about the operation, as though there wasn't time to do all that was needed. I think threshing crews have a sense of dignity and importance imparted by the knowledge that so many are dependent on them for their daily bread.

I can't recall the name of the farmer who boarded me or the exact location of his farm. It was on Flatrock River, a few miles below the town of Rushville. I had heard exciting things about the smallmouth bass of the Flatrock, and I started to pack my fly rod. Father vetoed that on the grounds that it denoted a frivolous turn of mind ill-suited to the hard-working image I was supposed to present. But I smuggled a line and some hooks in my bag, and on the one Sunday I was there I caught bass with a willow pole and worms from the manure pile. One was a dandy, nearly fifteen-inches long.

But the clearest memory I have of those blazing, dusty days and chiggery-itchy nights is the springhouse. It was in a shady ravine a few yards behind the barn. The farmer had dug back into the bank until he reached the solid rock from which the spring flowed. Then he built a shallow trough about two feet wide and eight feet long to hold the water. He arched it all over with oak timbers and covered them with several feet of dirt. It was a cool cave set back into the hillside.

There the frothy, new milk cooled in shallow, granite pans, and the cream rose in a golden skim that would cling to your

George Denny

118

finger in a thick, ropy clot. Other jugs and jars held eggs and skimmed milk and buttermilk that was rich with yellow flecks. One small jar held the "starter," a mixture of dough, yeast, and sugar that would be used to leaven the next batch of home-made bread. The pans and crocks were covered with plates or pie tins held down by stones. This foiled small robbers like mice and chipmunks, but if someone forgot to close the door in the evening, racoons might manage a successful raid.

Cherries were kept there until it was time to make them into pies. Later in the season melons, berries, peaches, and plums stayed fresh and cool. After circulating through the trough, the water flowed into a small pool that was lined with mint. The outlet of that pool was choked with watercress.

When we came in from work the springhouse was our first stop. We held our wrists under the spring until they ached from the chill. Then we drank from the tin dipper, splashed water on our faces, and sat on the ledge and soaked up coolness until the dinner bell rang.

No doubt that farm has a freezer now, and possibly air conditioning, but I'll wager the old springhouse is still a popular place when the mercury soars.

Rabbits and Quail

Cottontails were the number-one target of Midwestern hunters when I was a boy. I expect they still are, but now I wouldn't shoot a rabbit. Don't press me for the reason or I will say it's because I fear tularemia, but that's not the whole truth. I no longer kill four-footed animals.

Until I was eighteen or twenty I hunted rabbits with the greatest of enthusiasm. Mother welcomed them for the table. I got a few with the .22 before Father gave me the shotgun on my thirteenth birthday. One or two of those I shot on the run, the rest I saw sitting and shot in their forms or as they stopped to look back at me after running a few yards. This would often happen on the opening days of the season.

Now and then as we hunted rabbits we might stumble into a covey of quail, and if we could bring one or two home it was a day to remember. Some of Father's sporting companions had bird dogs, and of course they frowned on rabbit hunting. One of those friends took him quail hunting, and father compounded the grievous error of shooting a rabbit as a bird dog chased it. What then happened I do not know, but Father came home much chastened and later he admitted the crime and warned me sternly about it.

On day Father brought home a pointer, a great rawboned beast named Dan. That dog did love to hunt. He hunted quail, rabbits, chickens, cats—anything he could find. We did get a few birds with him, but the cost was too much. Father paid for several chickens and one large goose, meanwhile doing everything possible to domesticate the brute. It was no use. He chased sheep one day, the farmer peppered him with birdshot, and we got rid of him.

After Dan we had a series of bird dogs, and one little pointer was a good one. I forget his name but will always remember one bit of his work. I took a long shot at a crossing bird, knocked it down, and saw it run up a hill and out of sight. We put the little pointer on trail, and he went over the hill and was gone for at least five minutes. He came back with the bird in his mouth and half-way down the hill he stopped and pointed. I moved in and a bird flushed and flew toward Father, who dropped it cleanly. The little dog came to me, gave me my bird, then went over and picked up Father's bird and gave it to him. Father bragged about that for years.

After we graduated to quail hunting we shot rabbits only when mother said she would like a stew. Then suddenly our Hoosier bunnies began to be afflicted with tularemia. We were told we could tell the sick ones by the white spots on their

Rabbits and Quail

livers, but were warned at the same time that we dare not open them to find the spots if we had briar scratches on our hands. Since our hands were already briar-scratched, we shot no more rabbits. I expect there are medicines to cope with tularemia today, but not then. Some hunters died from it.

I have already mentioned old Ruby, half-pointer, half-setter, and the finest bird dog we ever owned. Father called her a poinsettia. She loved to hunt but on her own terms. She went her way slowly and carefully, and I can't remember if she ever flushed a bird. She completely ignored other dogs. She would not honor their points. She would come up behind a dog on point, and when she caught the scent she would freeze. Mostly that was behind the pointer, as she had an exceptional nose. But sometimes she would not be satisfied with the other dog's analysis of the situation and would move in ahead and work it out to her own satisfaction. Failure to back is of course considered a serious fault, and father did his best to break her of it. It was no use; she as much as told him, "I know a great deal more about quail than you do, so please just stay back there and let me handle things and we'll get along fine."

Soon Father had to agree. He stopped trying to direct her, and she never failed him.

I remember an afternoon about a week before the opening of the season when Father and several of his friends had an informal field trial. There were six dogs, as I recall, and they were all put down at once on a farm where we knew there were at least three coveys. Five took off across a big stubble field at full speed, working up wind. Ruby watched them go, uninterestedly, then turned in the opposite direction and ambled down a fence row about fifty yards. She wriggled through a fence into a weed field and immediately came on point. The other dogs were so far away we didn't try to get them up to back. Father

George Denny

and I flushed the covey and it was a big one; at least twenty birds. They made for cover along a creek bank a quarter of a mile away. We called in the other dogs, and they worked it out. They made two or three good finds, but the rest of those birds they flushed. It was a hot, dry day, so they had some excuse.

But they didn't move them all. Ruby came poking along a few minutes later and cracked down on three more, one at a time, and held them perfectly until we kicked them out.

A little later in the afternoon she found another covey. Two of the other dogs honored her point, but a third one blundered in ahead and flushed. Ruby watched that dog chase the birds, then turned and trotted away. Father called and whistled to no avail. She gave him a disgusted look and kept going. It was as though she said, "I'll waste no more time here with those stupid animals."

And she didn't. She went back to our car, curled up by it, and went to sleep.

We acquired Ruby when she was six or seven years old, and she hunted for us until she was fourteen or fifteen. What she lacked in speed she made up in bird sense, and she acquired more of that as she aged and slowed. She always knew where birds would be at any given time of day. Younger dogs might sometimes beat her to a covey find, but from then on she was the very best. No dog could match her work on singles. Father's hunting companions often called in their dogs after a covey rise and kept them on leash so Ruby would not be distracted while finding the scattered birds.

I know now that those hunts with old Ruby were priceless experiences and that I may never see their equal again. Quail hunting with a good dog is the best field sport I've ever enjoyed, and the dog work is a great part of that pleasure. And Robert White is a worthy opponent and a gentleman, and his wife is a

Rabbits and Quail

lady. Give them some shelter from hawks and foxes, leave them a little grain from your harvest, spare three or four pairs from each covey for seed, and they will prosper. They will cheer you with their happy mating song in the spring, keep down the insect pests that attack your crops, and then reward you with some of the finest upland shooting in the world each fall. And to top it all, they will bless your board in a manner that only jacksnipe and woodcock can match. Pheasant can't compare.

For quail buffs, only one day of the year really matters and that is when the season opens. Many, curious, and cunning are the devices used to keep that day holy. Judges look far ahead to keep dockets clear. Doctors and lawyers book no appointments. The butcher, baker, and candlestick-maker turn the business over to the help. In some rural areas town halls and courthouses are closed.

Memories of some of those hunts are still sharp. One miserably cold and rainy day in the hills below Bedford we were suddenly ringed by five grim-faced men with rifles. We had stumbled onto a moonshine still in full operation. It was a tight thing for a few seconds, but our native guide persuaded them we weren't revenuers and wouldn't even know how to find the place again. Then he suggested Father buy a bottle so they would feel we were part of the act. Father gave them two dollars for a pint Mason jar filled with a colorless liquid. As soon as we were out of their sight he opened it, smelled it, made a face, and poured it on the ground. Our guide shouted in horrified dismay at what he called a great waste of good moonshine. He barely spoke to us the rest of that day.

One evening Gene Miller and I were walking back to the car after a frustrating day. Two coveys had flushed wild far ahead of what seemed to be careful dog work. We had not found many singles, and those we did get up we couldn't hit.

George Denny

124

We had only three or four birds and should have had many more.

In the middle of the lane we were following was a small pile of hay fallen from a farm wagon. Gene's big pointer passed it, then twisted around and pointed with a quivering intensity that could not be gainsaid. I reached under the hay and pulled out a big cock bird, apparently in perfect health. I was tempted to wring his neck and add him to my small take, but that unsporting impulse didn't last long. I tossed him in the air, and he flew away, untouched, as we emptied our guns in wry acknowledgment to a day when we couldn't do anything right.

But there were good days, too. One I won't forget is the time I first got a limit. I was hunting with Willis Adams. We didn't get into the field until the middle of the afternoon, but Ruby found a big covey not fifty yards from the car, and we both doubled on the rise. As we were working out the singles we got into another covey. It was that kind of day. As dusk deepened I needed only one more for a limit. A single flushed wild and flew down a dark ravine. That was an unlucky bird. I could hear it but not see it until it angled across the white trunk of a huge sycamore. A snap shot brought it down, and Ruby found it for me.

I moved from bobwhite country more than two decades ago, and I have missed them. The desert quail don't taste as good, and they run too fast for my aging shanks. The valley quail of central and northern California are fair to good eating, but they won't hold well to a point and they fly into trees; a most unsporting habit. I hunt them now and then but without any great enthusiasm.

To me, in all outdoor sport there is no excitement like the seething ferment that builds to an almost unbearable pitch as I walk in behind pointing dogs, wondering when the covey will

Rabbits and Quail

explode. That is the moment of truth. Some November, if I keep my health, I'll throw the gear in the car and head east. I hear there are lots of bobwhite in Missouri. If I can't find them there, I'll keep going—Tennessee, North Carolina, Georgia. I'll drive the back roads until I come to a small town with a couple of pointers asleep on the porch of the general store. There I'll stay until I persuade someone to take me bobwhite hunting.

Since writing the above I have moved East and hunted bobwhite. I opened the season in Indiana with Bill Sully, in a spot where there were known to be at least three covies, but in spite of what appeared to be careful dog work by Sully's pointer Beau, we found not one bird. Plenty of sign—big, fresh roosts—just an off day.

I phoned my friend Hank Weed who had recently retired from his position in Detroit and naturally gravitated to the city where he was born and raised, Savannah, Georgia. He'd had some fine hunts for duck, woodcock and grouse since I last saw him about thirty years ago, but he hadn't hunted bobwhite since we last tried for them in Indiana that many years before.

"Come right down," he insisted. "I have no dogs yet and haven't had time to line up any good territory but we'll hunt on one of the game farms."

So I did and we did. And as I say in a later chapter, I have no compunction about paying for good shooting. It takes a rich man these days to afford the dogs, handlers, land and other necessities for the sort of hunting we used to take for granted thirty or forty years ago. I'm not rich so I expect that much of my gunning from now on will be on game farms or some of the public shooting lands.

Hank took me to a preserve near Statesboro, Georgia. We hunted just one morning; about three hours. We knocked down forty birds with seventy-one shells. One or two the dogs didn't

George Denny

126

find, mostly because when we would start after a cripple we'd run into another covey and lose track of the down bird in the ensuing excitement. I've never had better bobwhite shooting and, as Hank said, the percentage of birds down to shells expended wasn't too bad for a couple of old coots who hadn't hunted quail for many years. I shot the little Ithaca double and Hank a Parker given to his father by his grandfather in 1892. Yes, it has Damascus barrels, but Hank has been shooting it for years with light loads and fears not, despite the qualms of those who do not have his faith in Parkers.

All the old thrills were there—the dogs making game and then cracking down on point, the trembling, breathless approach, and then the sudden rise. I'll never be able to stay calm in that sequence of events. Hit or miss, it's the greatest pleasure I've ever had in the field.

Mixed Bag

A high-school teacher once asked my class to write a composition telling which of the four seasons we preferred, and why. I chose spring and rhapsodized at length about the escape from winter, the blooming of the red-bud and dogwood, the first try for bass, the first rusty swing at a golf ball, and so on. I didn't know about morel mushrooms at that time, and certainly they are a big plus for spring. Most of the class chose to write about that season, with fall a poor second and summer and winter trailing.

But now I find my thoughts going back to some of the Indian-summer days of autumn. One is especially sharp in me-

mory. It was the opening day of duck season, and Hank Weed and I had been looking forward to it. The northern flights were not down, but we knew of a slough in a cornfield near White River, south of town, and it yielded two brace of fat mallards. Those ducks had been raised there and had never been hunted. They flew from one end of the slough to the other, and we chose our shots, taking only drakes, before they got the message and took off.

On the way back to the car we flushed a big covey of quail and marked the spot carefully against the opening day a few weeks hence.

I remembered another slough near Cloverdale where I had seen a brood of mallards the year before. As we angled toward it on side roads we saw a grove of chestnuts that had escaped the blight and gathered half a bushel. A few miles farther on black walnuts littered the roadside. As we loaded them in the car trunk a brash, young gray squirrel scolded us for stealing his winter stores, and we added him to our bag.

The Cloverdale slough held no ducks, but from its marshy margins we walked up half a dozen jacksnipe and were fortunate to get three. If there is anything more sudden and unpredictable then the rise and flight of a jacksnipe, I am not aware of it. Another unexpected dividend from that spot was a huge tangle of wild grape vines, and we picked enough of their tiny

Mixed Bag

fruit to make many a glass of a jelly that can't be found in stores.

It was still not time for lunch, and we headed north to Sugar Creek. We stopped at a crossroad store and bought cheese, crackers, little tins of sausage, and a bottle of milk topped with rich cream. How long since you have seen heavy cream on your milk?

We ate that lunch on the bank of Sugar Creek at a spot we called Seven Springs. It was far from any road, in a heavy forest of hardwood. Not many knew the place, and those who did respected its quiet and beauty enough to keep it pristine. The springs issued from a rocky ledge, and several of them combined to form a brooklet that was choked with watercress. One gushed out over a ledge seven or eight feet high, so that we could stand under it on hot days and take a tingling shower.

It wasn't hot enough for a shower that day. It was perfect; the frosty dawn had warmed to a languid, lazy noon. We ate our lunch and lapsed into a doze.

But not for long. A whistle of wings jerked us to attention, but we reached for our guns too late as a small bunch of teal swept by. That reminded us that the day was young and there was sport still to be had. We left with all the watercress we could carry and added it to the loot in the trunk of the car. Downstream a few miles were several tangles of willows where I had seen woodcock in years past. We moved a few but it was hard work. They were flushing wild, but they didn't fly far and we finally worked out a system. One beat out the dense thickets while the other skirted the edges and took the shot as the bird topped the willows. It took us most of the afternoon to get two apiece.

As we rested on the bank of Sugar Creek after these happy exertions a fan of minnows broke the quiet surface ahead of a

George Denny

130

feeding bass. There just happened to be a flyrod in the car, and in no time I had two respectable smallmouths. As I played the second one a pair of mallards came over, and this time Hank was ready. He dropped one at my feet.

We found more black walnuts and a grove of ripe pawpaws. The persimmons weren't quite ready; they needed another sharp frost or two. A farmer's roadside stand offered fresh cider for thirty cents a gallon and a sack of mixed Jonathans and Grimes Goldens for ten cents. Pumpkins in his field reminded us that Halloween was not far distant. He refused payment for the two big ones we put in the back seat. The trunk was nearly full.

And to top off that fruitful day we stopped at a little momma-poppa grocery store on the outskirts of Crawfordsville. Momma ran the store, and poppa hunted and fished and raised hound dogs. But he was best known for his skill at catching large turtles from nearby waterways. Sure enough, he had made a good haul the day before, and we bought several pounds of the white snapping turtle steak that many prefer to veal.

As we drove home in the dusty twilight a harvest moon hoisted her golden corpulence over the mellow countryside. Indiana was dead ripe.

Hot Creek

Bill Lawrence and I disagreed on just one point. He wouldn't let me use nymphs or wet flies in his trout stream. Dry flies only in Hot Creek, he decreed, and no hooks larger than size 12. That's it—no argument. If you don't like my rules, fish elsewhere.

Hot Creek drains the Mammoth Lakes country and joins the Owens River about thirty miles northwest of Bishop, California. On the way down the slopes it is a brawling torrent that supports few trout. On the floor of the valley it furnishes water for a trout hatchery and below that, for about two miles, it flows through the Hot Creek Ranch, formerly owned by Lawrence. Just below the ranch are hot springs that give the creek its name and make the water too warm for trout. So it is that Hot Creek Ranch had virtually all the good fishing on the entire creek.

And it is good fishing; some declare the best they have ever experienced. The water is alkaline and full of weeds, and they shelter fine crops of insect larvae. And Bill didn't allow wading. You could cross his stream only on the footbridge or at a couple of gravelly spots farther down. Those weeds must not be disturbed.

The stream holds browns and rainbows. They are mostly wild trout from natural spawning, but it is generally believed that some of the crop came from the fish hatchery, just upstream. It was whispered that Bill contributed a case of Scotch for the Christmas party at the hatchery, and in return some pond gates were left open to let fish find their way down to Bill's water. Whatever the reason, the ranch stretch was rich with trout, and some were whoppers—ten pounds and more.

When I first fished there, circa 1951, Bill's rules were more liberal. Above the footbridge, wives, children, and beginners could use bait or hardware. But in a year or so he changed that to dry fly only, and there was no arguing about it. I tried. I pointed out that nymphs or wet flies fished upstream and allowed to drift back in a natural float, as described by Skues, was a most delicate and difficult way to present a lure. Dry fly fishing is crude and clumsy by comparison. The day of the Halford-type purist was long gone, I argued.

Bill countered with the statement that a good dry-fly man could bring fish to the surface under nearly any conditions. I wanted to debate that point, but it was no use. Dry fly or nothing, the man said.

And so, because it was such wonderful water, I obeyed his rules. Almost always, that is. How could any red-blooded trout fisherman keep from clipping the wings from his dry fly and spitting on it to make it sink when the water churned with bulging fish? But Bill, wherever you are and if you ever read this confession, I assure you that any fish I took by such dubious

Hot Creek

methods were carefully returned. In fact most that I caught there were returned. Now and then I would keep one ot two for lunch. I never took any home, but I take no credit for that. I feel that if you can't eat trout within an hour or two of the time they're caught, forget it.

The fishiest spots in the creek were in and near the weed cover. In places the entire width, bank to bank, was weedy. In such places a few channels would be kept open by the force of the flow. In most cases they were only a few inches wide.

How do you throw a dry fly into a narrow channel so it will float a foot or two without drag? In most of these places the water was fairly fast. The obvious approach is from directly below. From there even a beginner could make a fair presentation. But remember, no wading. The cast had to be made from the bank, usually at something near a right angle.

There were a few places where the channels were close enough to the bank for a fly to be dapped. At times this was a deadly approach. The fly could be made to dance an inch or so over the water like a live insect, and when it was lowered to the surface there was usually something there to greet it. Sometimes the trout jumped for it.

But soon the channels that could be reached by dapping from the bank were pretty well fished out. New methods had to be found to float a fly without drag in a narrow run with a fairly fast current and up to thirty feet from either bank. Dan Layman and I finally figured one out. We tied a light thread to a leader about three feet above the fly. We stood on opposite banks, one holding the end of the thread, the other the fly rod. The thread held the line and a section of the leader free of the water and allowed the fly to be worked along the channels; a partnership dapping technique.

George Denny

134

When a fish was hooked the man with the thread let it drop and the one with the rod tried to lead the fish out of the weeds. We got a lot of rises but not many trout. Usually the weeds prevailed. If there was much wind, it was difficult to steer the fly to the right spot. When the thread was dropped it might tangle in the weeds and break, and if not, there was the problem of getting it back across the stream, since we couldn't wade. It wasn't a very practical method, and I don't think we would have persisted with it much longer even if Bill hadn't come along, taken a scornful look, and told us to stop it.

"Don't gang up on my fish," he said. "Why don't you learn to cast to those runs?"

"Impossible," I said. "You get immediate drag."

"Wait right here," he said. He went to his trailer, came back with his fly rod, and proceeded to put on the damnedest exhibition of fly casting I have ever seen. He false casted until he had out a lot more line and leader than was needed to reach the channel we had been working. Then with some sort of leg-erdemain that still amazes and eludes me, he dropped his tiny fly in the channel with several feet of loose coils of leader above it. I remember that his first cast didn't satisfy him, and he picked it up immediately. He did the same with the second try, but on the third the fly and several loose coils of leader fell into that narrow run, and the fly floated down freely for about two feet before a trout took it.

He coaxed that fish out of the weeds—a fourteen-inch brown—and attacked another, even narrower channel farther down. This time it took him five or six tries to make the presentation he wanted, but as soon as the fly floated naturally for a foot or two he hooked another fish. That one flopped off in the weeds. A minute later he landed and released a twelve-inch

Hot Creek

rainbow, and that fish was taken from a channel not ten inches wide and twenty-five feet from the bank.

"That's how it's done," said Bill, with a mean grin. "Nothing to it." And he stalked off leaving us with our mouths open.

We tried to learn that technique, Lord knows we tried. I haven't been to Hot Creek for years but Dan has. Maybe he has mastered it by now. I haven't, but I'm still trying. Whenever I find a narrow run with weeds on both sides I work at it. Once or twice I've felt that I was about to solve the problem, and I do think I'm getting close. I remember that Bill waved his rod back and forth at a great rate and had a lot more line in the air than was needed to reach his target. He would snap the rod back, then start the forward motion before the line straightened out behind him. It seemed to me that by his rapid whippings he restricted the backward and forward motion of the fly to only a few feet and made it stay at the apex of a sort of pyramid of line and leader that formed above him. His rod moved so fast it was almost a blur. It was a most awkward-looking performance, a far cry from the graceful backing and forthing usually associated with false casting. But at the height of these unseemly vibrations he would stop the rod motion and the fly and loose coils of leader would drop to the water. They didn't always fall where he wanted them; far from it. Sometimes it took a dozen or more tries. The miracle is that he was ever able to do it.

I never caught one of Bill's monsters. A three-pound brown and a slightly smaller rainbow were my best. In 1961 my friend Woods Caperton caught a brown that weighed 11 pounds, four ounces, on a size-16 male Adams. His rod was a seven and one-half foot split bamboo Orvis. And I believe that fish was tops in one class of the *Field & Stream* contest that year.

George Denny

136

Hot Creek was a fine laboratory for angling experiments. I first read Hewitt's account of his Neversink Skater fly about 1952 and immediately went to Russ Peak's place, in Pasadena, to see if he had any. He had, and they were made by Ashley, Hewitt's son. They were beautiful flies, tied on light size-16 hooks, with long, stiff hackle, just as the old master described them. Russ wouldn't sell me those, but he had splendid duplicates.

Afternoons at Hot Creek are usually windy, and that's when I tried the Skaters. I rigged up with a long, light leader and thirty feet of linen backing tied to my fly line. It was much the same as the thread-line method that used to be popular on English streams.

That afternoon the wind was so strong I had to lower the rod tip to within a few feet of the water before the big fly would touch the surface. Then trout would chase it but seldom take hold. It would often be whipped back into the air just as a fish rose for it. After an hour the wind became so strong and gusty I could not control the fly, but in that time I hooked three trout and landed two, one a twelve-inch rainbow. And there had been many unsuccessful efforts, some by big fish. One came halfway out of water as the fly was whipped away, and I got a good look at him. That fish was at least two feet long. I tried the Skaters another time or two, and they always provoked some action, but the big fish were never able to connect. The stiff hackles of the big fly seemed to hold the little hook away from their eager mouths.

At other times I tried tiny midges on size-18 and 20 hooks, and they moved good-sized fish. But even with Polaroid glasses I had trouble following their float, and one time Bill came by and watched for a moment and sternly told me there was a good

Hot Creek

reason I couldn't see my fly, because it was a wet fly and you cut that out right now, Denny.

Then I went to a large, bushy fly that Bill immediately challenged. He asked to see it, but in spite of the fact that it was almost as large as a half dollar the hook was a legal size 12, and I had bent down the barb with my little pliers. That big fly took fish and it must have been from curiosity, since there were no naturals even slightly resembling it.

Hot Creek Ranch is managed now by Lee Willardson and the rickety old cabins that we used to endure for the sake of the great fishing have been replaced by modern, all-electric housekeeping cottages. And Lee has not relaxed Bill's strict rules by one iota. Dry flies only—you earn your fish and it's not always easy. And spinning tackle is of course worthless under these conditions, for which the good Lord be praised.

On rereading this I see I may have been uncharitable to Bill Lawrence. I disagreed, and still do, with his stand on nymph and wet fly fishing, but it was his water and his right. And I will always remember with awe and respect the way he could fish those narrow channels.

Mountain Trout

To an angler whose trout lore had been accumulated in the peaceful pools, smooth glides, and occasional riffles of the Michigan waters, the foaming, boulder-studded streams of New Mexico and Colorado were puzzling, to put it mildly. I made notes of the fishing on that trailer trip in 1936. They reflect awe, wonder and plaintive surprise at the unfamiliar conditions. The first entry reads:

"June 2. Pecos River, above the town of Pecos, about 25 miles east of Sante Fe, New Mexico. Water high, very fast but clear. Snow still melting on peaks. No place for dry fly. Huge rocks. Fell down twice, tore waders. Two small rainbows and brown on wet flies. Lost big one."

You've heard of the Pecos. Outlaws tried to cross it ahead of the posse. If they did, they were safe. There was no law west of the Pecos until Judge Roy Bean set up his kangaroo court at the town of Langtry, so named because of his yearning for the actress Lily Langtry. We crossed the river near that town, and at the top of the rise on the west bank a tarantula stood in the middle of the road and contested our passage. It was a fitting introduction to the Texas badlands. But down there the Pecos had no fish appeal. Only in New Mexico, in the shadow of the Truchas peaks of the Sangre de Cristo range will you find trout.

I parked at a wide place in the road and scrambled down a rocky slope through pines and alders. It was my first trouting trip of the season, and the strange weakness that overtakes me at such times, turning my knees to rubber and afflicting my fingers with a maddening palsy, made a trembling, breathless task of the tackle-assembling ceremony. Then I spent long minutes looking for a stretch where the little Brown Hackle could be floated even for a second or two. There were no such places; the churning waters devoured dry flies. I substituted a small bee-bodied streamer, and went at it wet and downstream.

On the third or fourth cast, with the fly skipping the riffles like a scared minnow, a speedy little rainbow no longer than ten inches took hold and snapped the leader point like thread. Stupid of me to risk 4X gut in such furious water. I cut the leader back to about 2X and tied on a larger streamer.

Twice in the next few casts I saw trout dash at the fly and miss. Then one connected solidly, and the next few seconds passed approximately as follows: a couple of jumps toward the far bank; an underwater dash back to the deepest, swiftest part

George Denny

140

of the channel; a series of tugs and darts that forced me to give line. As I tried to follow downstream I slipped and fell. I sat in eight inches of icy water that crested up my backside and began to fill my waders. As I struggled up I slipped again, and my hat fell off. I grabbed it and crawled ashore on my knees, hat in one hand and rod in the other. The fish was still on, resting in a backwater. He fled out of that into the current. It was like flying a kite in a hurricane, but I let the rod take the shocks, everything held, and the next time I got that trout to the surface I skated it across and up the bank. Not quite eleven inches of fat rainbow, cold and firm and silvery as an icicle.

There was water in my waders and a rip in one knee. I sloshed up to the car, changed pants, and put on hip boots. In water like that, boots are all that are needed. You can't navigate safely if it's over your knees, and boots will remind you not to try. And felt soles are a must. Those mountain torrents are paved with round, slick stones.

My experience with that first one made me wonder if I was adequately armed for the contest. If an eleven-incher could give me that much trouble, what would a big one do to my little rod? In that sissy frame of mind I tried two or three more bends (the straight stretches were too intimidating) and landed two more little ones. Then I came to a spot where the current smashed head-on into a wall of sheer rock, forming a large eddy. There I hooked the big one.

At first that trout ignored me. He made a slow turn around the pool, then sank to the bottom and sulked. I got below him and applied all the pressure I dared. I got no response. I came back even with him and heaved a big rock just above his hold. That moved him. He went out through the tail of the pool and into white water. It had been years since I checked the backing

Mountain Trout

on my reel, and I suddenly feared it might not be as strong as the heavy leader point. Rather than take a chance I lowered the rod tip and clamped down while there was still fly line on the reel. The hook straightened out. How big was that fish? I never saw him and should not hazard a guess. All right, if you insist. Nearer six pounds than three.

It was enough for that day. I was pluckbroke. The natives had warned me that the Pecos would not be friendly water that early in the season. Give it about ten more days and most of the snow melt will be down river, they said.

I waited that long for a second try, and the water was much more to my liking. There was a hatch of big willow flies, and trout were taking them and something smaller. I had nothing close to an imitation of the willow flies except a grasshopper fly, but that was good enough. But after I had netted three or four small ones a big one wrapped the leader around a snag on the far bank. It was my only 'hopper fly, and nothing else worked. Another angler came downstream with a good basket of fish. His method was simple. The bushes were crawling with the big

willow flies, and he used them for bait with a split shot on a short leader. He dapped the natural fly into runs and pockets along the bank. More often that not the fish stole his bait, but there were plenty more. I saw him try four or five times in one small eddy behind a rock before he hooked the thief.

I tried that dapping for awhile with absolutely no success. They took the bait every time. Then a hatch of what looked like big mosquitos gave me an excuse to go back to the dry artificials. My catch of eight that day averaged about nine inches, and the largest was not eleven. Perfect for the frying pan.

On a third trip I found a small irrigation dam that backed the water into a smooth flow for a couple of hundred feet. On my first try at this stretch with a yellow-bodied gray hackle I had five rises and landed four trout—three browns and a rainbow. The fifth one found a submerged snag. I had been fishing downstream with a streamer, and my leader was only eight feet long and tapered to 2X. None of those four fish was longer than nine inches.

I added 3X and 4X tippets, making the leader eleven feet long. I fished that stretch again with the same fly. This time I rose five trout and landed four, as on the first try. But they averaged at least two inches longer. The largest crowded thirteen inches. There may have been other factors beside leader size and length operating toward that end, but I doubt it.

As I was taking down my rod an angler came upstream, fishing the broken water below the dam. I watched him take a rainbow from a boiling stretch where it seemed no fish could live. He would pick a spot, usually an eddy behind a rock, and slap down his flies "hard enough to knock the water out of the river," as he put it.

"How do you know when you have a hit? Do you see them or feel them?" I asked.

George Denny

144

"Sometimes I see it flash," he said. "Sometimes I see the leader check. But mostly I strike on suspicion."

The faster the water, the shorter the line, he explained. Often he lowered the flies directly into a run or pocket. His dropper was a black-bodied affair with a wisp of soft, gray hackle. The stretcher looked like a Silver Doctor. Both were tied on size-10 hooks.

"The browns like the dark fly and the rainbows want color," he said.

"Do you lose many after they hit?" I asked.

"About half."

"Wish I knew how to handle wet flies in this water," I said.

"I saw you taking them up there with a dry fly," he said. "I wish I knew that game."

"It's easy, much easier than what you're doing," I said.

"Not for me," he said. So there you are.

I would like to forget the trip to the Rio Grande. My notes say:

"From Sante Fe north about eighty miles to the canyon just south of the Colorado border. Waited until last week in June for water to clear. Fish only in riffles, according to local dope. Wasted an hour with dry flies, then went to small bucktail, black and silver body and gray hair wings. Got several smashing hits from good fish but lost them all. Two broke leader, others threw hook. Big, fast water.

"Finally hooked one solid. Fine rainbow, sixteen inches or better. Jumped twice when hooked, then four more jumps while taking all the fly line and much backing. Chased him down to a pool where he sulked on bottom. Came up with head covered with moss and docile as a kitten. Led him up close and just as I was about to net him the hook came away."

Mountain Trout

On that sad note the entry ends, but I remember that later in the evening I hooked two smaller fish, and they both escaped by one means or another. Not my day. I'd like to try that spot again and see if I could redeem myself. I'd have something heavier than a three-ounce rod. But instead of a lovely stretch of wild river with no sign of civilization I might find a pulp mill or chemical plant spewing poison into the water. Or maybe that stretch would be drowned by an Army Corps of Engineers' dam. I'd rather remember it as it was, humiliating defeat and all.

Our next stop was Boulder, Colorado. The camp was on Boulder Creek, and I parked the trailer with its stern actually overhanging the water. There, in the next two weeks, I learned something of the art of handling a fly in fast water. A wet fly, of course. Any pools or glides where a dry fly could float for more than a few feet were hard to find.

After two or three days with only a couple of recognizable hits and no fish I began to question the existence of trout in that water. I tried streamers downstream and nymphs and wet flies up and down. But the natives assured me there were plenty of trout in Boulder Creek, and I kept at it. In a few days I somehow began to get the knack. I can't explain it. I have no idea what subtle change in my method made the difference, but I began to take trout with the same flies and from the same spots I had tried earlier. And there it was again, the lesson I had learned years before on the Michigan streams. You learn to fish by fishing.

George Denny

146

On to Pucklechurch

When I was seventeen—give or take a few months—I picked up a slim volume from the sidewalk stall of a second-hand book store. I had never heard of Dame Juliana Berners, and her *Treatyse of Fysshyng wyth an Angle*, but I noted the date—1885—and saw it was a reprint of part of a book that was first issued in 1496. I puzzled through a few lines of the old English spelling where *v* was *u* and *i* was *j* and noted that it described the dressing of a number of artificial flies. That sold it. I had only a day or two earlier bought my first fly-tying vise. I gladly paid the asking price of fifteen cents.

Since that rich discovery I've never been able to pass a second-hand book store. My latest find is a reprint of *The Secrets of Angling*, by John Dennys. The first edition was issued in 1613, forty years before *The Compleat Angler*. Dennys was the grandson of the Lord of the Manor of Oldbury-sur-Montem and had holdings in the county of Gloucester. He was a devoted angler and more than just a competent poet. His book is all in rhyme, and though it can't contend with that of his neighbor and contemporary William Shakespeare, it surpasses the efforts of many Elizabethan versifiers. Thomas Westwood, who wrote the Introduction to my 1883 edition, has this to say:

"The English poets of the Art of Angling perplex us neither with their multitude, nor their magnitude. To some three or four of them may be assigned a place—shall we say midway, by courtesy?—on the ledges of Parnassus. . . . Foremost among the select few, by right of seniority, and perhaps by poetic right as well, we have 'I. D.'—"

That's our man, John Dennys. *J.* was still *I.* a hundred years plus after Dame Juliana. And not only does his verse charm us with impeccable meter, quaint philosophy, and sound angling advice, it also raises the question of who first wrote of fishing the dry fly. As an amateur in pursuit of that truth, I find in Dennys's verses strong evidence that he might have claimed the honor.

It has been generally accepted that the dry fly was first used in the second quarter of the nineteenth century. I am one of a host of Haig-Brown aficionados (forgive the pun) who think that his *A River Never Sleeps* is one of the happiest and soundest books on angling to appear in the last four or five decades. In it he states:

"Pulman's *Vade Mecum of Flyfishing* is the first book that sets forth clearly and unequivocally the basis of modern dry-fly technique; an upstream cast and the drift of a fly to a rising trout."

I've not questioned that statement until recently. But hark:

> *See where another hides himselfe as slye,*
> *As did* Acteon, *or the fearfull Deere;*
> *Behinde a withy, and with watchfull eye*
> *Attends the bit within the water cleere,*
> *And on the top thereof doth moue his flye,*
> *With skilfull hand, as if he liuing were.*

George Denny

That's our withy skulker, John Dennys, writing early in the seventeeth century, some two hundred and forty years before Pulman. A few stanzas later he tells us that fish seek food on the bottom, "Or at the top of water, streame or flood." And for the latter he advises us to to fish with no lead (weight) at all,

> *Or else vpon the top thereof ye shall*
> *With quicker hand, and with more ready skill*
> *Let fall your flye, and now and then remoue,*
> *Which soone the Fish will finde and better loue.*

Isn't he saying that with care and dexterity the angler should be able to keep his fly on the surface? But most significant, most telling are these two lines. Think well on them.

> *And on the top thereof doth moue his flye,*
> *With skilfull hand, as if he liuing were.*

I remember the first time a twisted leader uncoiled and gave my fly a little hop. No sooner had I thought, how lifelike it must seem, than the best trout of the day backed my judgment with a slashing rise. Failing twisted leaders, I have many times since then attempted the tiny twitch that is so deadly when accomplished without appreciable drag. And here we find Dennys describing that trick and no doubt using it in the late fifteen and early sixteen hundreds.

Was he dry fly fishing? One thing is certain: that deceit can only be attempted with a floating fly. It may be deduced that he was dapping instead of casting, but where shall we draw that line as long as the fly is dropped above and floats down to a rising fish?

No angler could fail to note and plan to profit by the care-

On to Pucklechurch

149

less greed with which trout sometimes attack floating insects. Surely even before Dennys's time fishermen tried to dry their flies and keep them on top as long as possible while trout were gulping surface prey. Granting this, I suggest that the art of dry fly fishing was not developed sooner because of inadequate tackle. I'll wager if Dennys's rod had been as light and quick as those enjoyed by Pulman and Halford two hundred and fifty years later, he would have been false casting even the horsehair lines of his day and singing in much more detail of the delights of fishing a floating fly.

And now, some months after writing the above, I am brought up short by reading *A History of Fly Fishing for Trout,* by John Waller Hills. In it he says:

"Fly fishing is not mentioned . . . in his much quoted but still beautiful poem, the *Secrets of Angling,* published in 1613."

Since Hills could hardly have failed to note the verses quoted earlier I assume he thought Dennys referred to the use of natural, not artificial, flies. That he may be correct is evident in two lines I found on a careful rereading of the poem. Among "other fishing tooles" recommended is

> *A little Box that couered close shall lye,*
> *To keepe therein the busie winged Flye.*

Difficult as it is to fault a scholar like Hills, let's remember that artificial flies were used even before Dame Juliana wrote of them in the fifteenth century, and surely an angler as devoted to his sport as Dennys knew of them. I want to believe he was referring to artificials in those verses.

G. P. R. Pulman may have been the first to write at some length on the use of the dry fly, but he wasn't the first to mention them, even if we discount any claim made for Dennys. Let's

George Denny

150

look at *Salmonia, or Days of Fly Fishing,* by Sir Humphry Davy. The first London edition is dated 1828. That antedates the Pulman first edition by thirteen years. Mine is Davy's first American edition, printed in Philadelphia in 1832. In it he says: "You see the alder fly is quite as successful as the May-fly; but here is a fish that has refused it, and because he has been feeding, glutton-like, on the May-fly: that is the fifth he has swallowed in a minute. Now I shall throw the drake a foot above him. It floats down and he has taken it."

Could that be plainer? Note the verb "throw." No dapping there. And we know he used an artificial, not a natural fly, because he describes the dressing of it on the preceding page. It seems that Pulman must at least share the honors.

Then there was James Ogden, the finest angler of his time if we credit his own word for it. In the preface of his book, *Ogden on Fly Tying,* devoted largely to his prowess with the rod and the excellence of his tackle, he declares: "It is well known that I am the inventor of Floating Flies, the Seat Basket and the Spring Folding Landing Net, which is so conveniently carried on the basket strap; also the celebrated Devil Killers, which have proved so deadly they have been prohibited on many streams."

That's what we must admire about Ogden; he sings not small. He was, it seems, a professional; a man who earned his bread by the angling skill that helped promote the sale of the fishing gear he manufactured. Not quite a gentleman by the standards of those times. In trade. In his little book published in 1879 he goes on to say: "Some forty years ago when I introduced my floating flies. . . ."

At the latest that would have him fishing dry in 1839, two years before Pulman wrote of it. And with all his conceit the man does make a good case. He tells how, when working a shy fish with

On to Pucklechurch

a cast of three flies, he would change the end fly so it would float for a throw or two and often do the job when wet flies failed.

"These observations were the cause of my introducing floating flies," he says, but we are looking for the first writings on the subject, and Ogden waited too long. And in any case Pulman must be moved to the head of this class because it was he who first advocated false casting, in the third edition of his *Vade Mecum of Fly-Fishing for Trout,* published in 1851.

Now back to Dennys's book. As a sort of fringe benefit I found this in the introduction: "... in the north Aisle of the Ancient Church of Pucklechurch is the burial place of the family of Dennys."

I went to the garden and read the passage to my wife, who was weeding japonicas, or some such green thumbery.

"So you see," I beamed, "we will have to go to Pucklechurch."

She didn't even look up.

"Dennys can always find an excuse to go fishing," she stated, "or is it grouse hunting this time?"

But the issue is not dead. A man owes something to an ancestor who loved to fish, if indeed John is one of mine. That I hope to determine when I visit Pucklechurch.

The best was yet to come. On the last page is the most intriguing part, set forth in the only verses Dennys did not write. In the Introduction, Westwood says:

"The fact of the second, third, and fourth editions being distinct is proved ... by variations ... in the leaf containing the mystical recipe—'Woulds't thou take fish?' Thus in the second edition we are told—

'This excellent recipe you may buy ready and truely made at the signe of the Black Lyon, an Apothecaries', in Paule's-Churchyard neare the Great South dore.'

George Denny

152

"In the third, we are referred for the same to the 'Signe of the Flying Horse an Apothecaries' in Carter Lane.' "

And on the last page—this charming puzzle:

Woulds't thou catch fish?
Then here's thy wish;
Take this receipt,
to annoynt thy Baite.

Thou that desir'st to fish with Line and Hooke,
Be it in poole, in Riuer, or in Brooke,
To blisse [sic] thy baite and make the fish to bite:
Loe, here's a meanes, if thou canst hit it right,
Take Gum of life, fine beat, and laid in soake,
In Oyle, well drawne from that which kils the Oake.
Fish where thou wilt, thou shall haue sport thy fill,
When twenty faile, thou shalt be sure to kill.

Probatum.

It's perfect and good,
If well understood;
Else not to be tolde
For Siluer or Golde.

B.R.

How about that? Let's take it a bit at a time. *Probatum* is a contraction of *probatum est* and means "it is proven." As for the initials after the last line, I have no clue. But did you note his warning to keep the secret?

What is the secret? What is gum of life? If we knew, we could no doubt beat it fine. What is oily and kills the oak? Mistletoe? I've asked doctors, apothecaries, alchemists, astrologers,

On to Pucklechurch

153

and a Ouija board. They do not know. This all smacks of Shakespeare's witch's brew, "Eye of newt and toe of frog," and I couldn't be more happily bemused by it.

I know there are divers scents, poisons, and extracts that are supposed to kill, fuddle, or attract fish. I've even seen ads in outdoor magazines that promise unbelievable results if you will bless your bait with their elixir. I've never given these claims much credence, feeling that if they were half as effective as advertised, no responsible publication would carry them.

Still, come to think of it, there was a doctor in San Diego who would promise friends a successful trip for marlin, sailfish, and the like. I have it from unimpeachable sources that he could make good that boast. He would use his potion only *in extremis;* when it appeared that the day might be a complete failure. Then he would take a small bottle of clear liquid from his tackle box and rig it to the stern of the boat so that a thin stream dripped into the sea. I am assured by more than one witness that fish would soon chase the boat and hit savagely at the baits. That was disturbing news, and I was glad to hear that the good doctor had sworn to take his secret to the grave.

And I also recall that in my home town of Indianapolis was a character called Chicken Gut Jones, who made magic with a noisome mux said to be compounded mostly of overripe poultry entrails. But there must have been more to it than that because many others tried to emulate his lure with all sorts of smelly efforts, and none succeeded. It was said that if a dollop of his mix was placed on the bank so that a few drops could trickle to the water, catfish would struggle up onto dry land in pursuit of it.

What to do about that secret recipe in Denny's book? I'd like to run it down if only to satisfy a raging curiosity. But if it proved to be as potent as claimed and somehow fell into unprincipled

George Denny

154

hands, I would regret the effort. Fish have a hard enough time these days, just dodging pesticides.

Just the same, Londoners mustn't be surprised to see me poking about in Carter Lane and Paule's-Churchyard near the Great South dore. Maybe those old drugstores, the Signe of the Flying Horse or the Black Lyon, are still in business. But if I find that formula in their old records I'll be tempted to spirit the page away and destroy it. After I try it, of course.

Then on to Pucklechurch.

Hair Frogs

My affair with the hair frog began many years ago, and it was love at first sight. On a lazy afternoon in early fall Bill Sully and I were fishing the Tippecanoe River a few miles above its junction with the Wabash. It was in 1930, give or take a year, and in those days the Tippy was one of the best smallmouth streams in Indiana, or in the entire Midwest, for that matter. Now it's dammed almost to death in the opinion of many of us cranky old codgers who preferred the miles of wadeable meander to any lake fishing.

The water was in fine shape, and the bass should have been putting on fat for the winter, but after a couple of hours with streamers and various spinner-and-fly combinations we had only one keeper. A few minutes after sunset we came to a quiet backwater where a hatch of large flies were hovering and dipping. As we watched, fish began to rise to them. I had no large dry flies and went to one of the cork-bodied poppers Will Dilg made famous.

Ten minutes later I had only a couple of half-hearted swirls to report while Sully had landed one good fish and was into another that got into heavy current where it couldn't be held. In the next pool down I helped him land a smallmouth that crowded four pounds. In the corner of its jaw was a lure the like of which I had never seen.

"Where'd you get that contraption?" I wanted to know.

"A tackle store in Noblesville sells them. They're tied by someone that lives near there. He calls them hair frogs."

It's possible that was one of the first hair frogs ever tied, and if so, I'd like to honor the inventor by naming him. On the other hand, he was probably only improving on a design taken from some other experimenter and might not be too proud of those early efforts. I still have one of the lot I bought next day at the Noblesville shop. It's poorly put together by comparison with later models. The deer-hair body is loosely tied and streamlined instead of being short and blunt. The legs are too short and are not cocked out and up. I like my hair frogs tied dense and tight with the body clipped up close to the shank of the hook. The legs should be about twice as long as the body, spread at around thirty degrees, and tilted up about forty-five degrees. These are personal preferences developed over the years, but there are other designs that seem to be as effective. Some have gaudy paint jobs with stripes and eyes laid on. I believe such embellishments are more attractive to fishermen than to fish.

I have fished hair frogs with hook sizes from 2 to 12, and in many colors. For years I favored yellows, greens, and an occasional red. Now I'm pretty sure that if the natural deer hair shade won't move fish, I'd better try another lure.

If the deer hair body is tied tight and hard, the frog can be kept buoyant by liberal applications of dry fly dope, and I used to take great pains to that end. I would even change frogs when they became waterlogged. Now I believe that makes them more attractive. A deer-hair frog, properly tied, will not sink no matter how sopping it gets, and a frog or mouse or even a big

Hair Frogs

157

beetle will be naturally deep in the water. I used to waste a lot of time trying to make frogs sit up on top like a cork.

Many times hair frogs have taken fish for me when other lures failed. Not long ago I was at a ranch where hunting and fishing is reserved for members of a sportsmen's club and their guests. My host frowned when I tied a small frog to my tapered leader.

"If that's a floating bug I'm afraid it won't get you much action until evening," he said. "I'm going to try down fairly deep for a while."

It was bright and warm and still, but the frog on a size-8 hook, fished just outside the shoreline weed beds, raised bass and bluegills all afternoon. Those bluegills were scrappier than the bigmouths. They'd plane down and away with that deep body, and the fly rod simply couldn't turn them until they tired. Two of them weighed more than a pound each.

In the meantime my host tried about every lure his light spinning tackle would handle, but he had no luck until dusk. Even then my frog did as well as his top-water plug.

I have already written of our six-month trailer trip. I took plenty of hair frogs, and they caught fish for me from Florida to the Rockies. We spent two weeks at the little town of Fairhope, Alabama, across the bay from Mobile. The hair frogs made good scores on the bass and bluegills—called trout and brim by the natives—in all the nearby ponds and creeks. I fished with several of the local anglers, and my frogs did as well as or better than their baits and casting lures nearly every time. I converted a couple of them to the fly rod and gave them so many of my stock of frogs that I had to send back to Indianapolis for more. At that time I believed that good hair frogs were tied only by a few Hoosiers. I found nothing that resembled them on that trailer trip that took us through fifteen states, and I looked

George Denny

carefully. Even today I find fly fishermen who have never heard of them, and many tackle shops have nothing like them. We moved from Indiana in 1949, and since then I have had to send back there for hair frogs more than once.

One evening we were picnicking on Mobile Bay near the estuary of a small stream. A fan of bait minnows broke water ahead of feeding fish. I had been working the creek that afternoon, and my fly rod was rigged and ready. I dropped the hair frog near one of the swirls, and it drifted in with the rising tide. I gave it a sharp twitch, and it popped and gurgled. I saw the riffle coming at it, and it startled me so that I struck too soon. But I dropped it right back in the same spot and this time something took it with a fine slurp.

At first that fish didn't know it was hooked. It made another pass at the minnows before deciding that the sting in its jaw was something to worry about. Then it headed for open water, and I'll never know what it was. I turned the first run near the end of the backing and had a moment of hope, but on the second run I had to clamp down, and the hook straightened out. It didn't jump, so it surely wasn't one of the small tarpon seen there occasionally.

Speaking of tarpon, an Indiana fisherman whose name I can't recall told me he had smashing sport on little tarpon—up to five or six pounds—in some borrow pits and canals in the Everglades. They took just about any fly rod lure he tossed at them but seemed expecially fond of his hair frogs, he reported. He also told of taking a twelve-pound largemouth on the frog.

We didn't get as far south as the Everglades, but I caught bass on the frog all through central Florida and back along the Gulf into Texas. I remember taking a two-pounder from a small lake not far from the Bok Singing Tower while the famous Belgian carillonneur played tunes for me.

One summer evening many years ago I was fishing the Little

South in Michigan a couple of miles above where it joins with the Middle Branch to form the Pere Marquette. I had a sandwich in my pocket, so I wouldn't have to go back to camp for dinner. That evening I was determined to stay on the stream until it was pitch dark, and that meant till near midnight. For years I'd heard about the huge brown trout that fed only at night. The natives said they sounded like pigs wallowing in the pools and that they ate only substantial chunks of meat like mice, young squirrels, and the like.

I first planned to try a hair mouse, then switched to my largest hair frog. A couple of bends below Octagon Castle was a long, fairly deep pool with a wide sand bar on one side that gave plenty of room for back casts. I reasoned there was little need for subtlety in the darkness, and the leader I prepared was only seven feet long and plenty strong—I thought.

I fished the pool with conventional tackle until it was too dark to see a White Miller, then sat on a log, ate my sandwich, and smoked a pipe until it was as dark as the pit.

As I worked slowly up into the pool with short casts I heard sucking rises that told of big fish working the surface. I wasn't aware of it when the trout took the frog. I tried to pick it up for another cast, and it wouldn't pick up. At first I thought I was snagged on the far bank, then the fish moved slowly up the pool and I knew I was into one of those pigs.

For long minutes that trout cruised easily around the lower part of the pool, apparently unaware of any danger. The pressure of my rod seemed to mean little or nothing to it. But I began to detect some pattern to the circling, and I made ready my net. Each pass brought him a bit closer, and finally I could see a dark form over the light sand bottom. I made a sweep with the net, and got his head in it. But the belly of my little net was only about twelve-inches long, and I swear that wasn't half the length of that trout.

George Denny

160

As I turned back to the bank I made a desperate attempt to lift and hold him in the net, but it was like trying to catch a greased pig in your hat. One great flop and he was out, and now he didn't like what was happening. He went through the riffle at the tail of the pool and may still be going. Fortunately the weak spot was in the leader, so I lost only a part of that and the frog. I know that trout was as long as my arm because when I tried to lift him in the inadequate net his tail slapped my face.

I waded slowly back to the sand bar, sat on the log, and lit my pipe with shaking hands. In a few minutes I recovered enough to rig up again, with help from a pen light, and in the next half hour I took two browns on a hair frog. One was over fourteen inches; the other nearly nineteen. The next day I retired that net in favor of one with a belly twice as long.

It's possible that any large floating lure would have done as good a job that night, but I doubt it. The hair frog moves more naturally in the water than any cork-bodied creation. I forgot to say that I was animating the frog with tiny twitches that night on the Little South.

Anglers who have had the good fortune to fish at Hot Creek Ranch, north of Bishop in eastern California, will usually agree that it may just be the finest dry-fly water in this nation. If you can't catch fish, it's your own fault because they are there in spectacular quantities. Credit for this excellent angling is largely due to Bill Lawrence, who owned the place for years and enforced his "dry-fly-only" rule with a beady eye. But now that Bill has sold out I'll admit to some research when his back was turned. I tried the hair frogs there.

Bill's rules forbade a hook larger than size 12. I had frogs tied on that hook size, and I started with one of them, feeling it was a technical violation at worst. Fished like a dry fly, with no motion or drag, the little frog went largely unnoticed. In several dozen

Hair Frogs

161

casts only two small fish splashed at it and neither was hooked. Results were better when I gave the frog some movement. I worked it through some riffles, now and then jumping it from crest to crest, and caught four keepers, none over ten inches. I hasten to add that all fish taken by those questionable methods were instantly returned.

Then I moved down to a deep bend known to shelter several large trout. I changed to a frog on a size-6 hook and a heavier leader. I cast into the head of the pool, let the frog drift down under the overhanging bank, and worked it back with little jerks. On the third or fourth try a heavy fish took it and retreated into the hole under the bank. I had plenty of leader, and I leaned into him with confidence, but after a few surges the hook came away.

Bill's return from town put an end to that investigation, but I had proved the point. Trout can be taken on the hair frog in the daytime. And those experiments confirm what many western anglers have long known, that trout can often be beguiled by flies given deliberate drag, especially in fast water. Haig-Brown tells how to do it with a fly tied with deer-hair body and wings, to float more surely in rough water. The cross-stream cast is allowed to straighten out downstream; then in the retrieve the fly is made to skip from wave to wave. If those Vancouver Island trout will attack a hair fly handled like that, they should find my hair frogs, legs pumping back and forth, even more seductive.

The hair frog can't be expected to compete with dry flies under normal conditions, but when conventional methods fail I give it a chance. An instance comes to mind. A few years ago I was exploring some side roads in Olympic National Park, in Washington. A small lake with marshy banks looked fishy, and I stopped there for lunch. Soon I saw a heavy swirl near some lily pads, and for the next half hour I tried that spot with every fly in

George Denny

the book. Once a fish followed a big brown nymph, and the glimpse I had made me want him badly.

I thought of the hair frog and then remembered I had needed one the day before and found I hadn't brought that particular box of lures. But I looked again and found one battered specimen with my streamer flies. One leg was nearly gone and the hook size was No. 6, a couple of sizes larger than I would have liked. But I dropped it by the pads, let it sit for five seconds, twitched it once, and the fish had it with a splash. He was sixteen inches of cutthroat, deep and fat, and with a back so dark green it was nearly black.

Beside the fish already mentioned I have caught rock bass, white bass, pickerel, yellow perch, and a couple of varieties of sunfish with my hair frogs. The Wabash River near Logansport used to be known for big bass. There is a riffle not far above the city where the river spreads out over a run pocked with rocks and ledges. It's wadeable, with care, though some of the scours behind the rocks are surprisingly deep. I fished that stretch one summer when the water was unusually low, and I think most of the better bass had dropped down into deeper pools. I caught two that were barely keepers, one on a black streamer behind a brass spinner and one on the frog. But the best fish of the evening took the frog as it was sucked under water by a swirl where the current boiled around the edge of a rock. When it didn't pop back to the surface at once I thought it was snagged. It was, in the lip of a channel cat that gave me a surprising battle before I netted its slender twenty inches. For my money a channel cat in cool water is as fine a scrapper for his weight as any bass, and better on the table.

I have tried to interest tailing carp with a hair frog once or twice but only succeeded in scaring them out of the shallows. The only reason I tried such an improbable ploy was that Jim Ross

Hair Frogs

assured me he had taken several carp on the frog, and they fought like bulldogs. He said the secret was to drop a small frog well ahead of a feeding carp and move it with the tiniest of jiggles. I must have cast too close to them, but I'll keep trying. A ten- or fifteen-pounder on a fly rod would be something.

One evening I was fishing a farm pond said to harbor a monster bigmouth. After I tried his haunts at the deep end with no success I changed to a small hair frog and went after the big bluegills that were taking surface flies in the weeds. One cast dropped on a lily pad an inch or two from the shore. I let it sit there for a few seconds. Suddenly it disappeared, and there was no disturbance in the water. Puzzled, I raised the rod tip and there was a great splash about four feet out from the bank. After quite a hassle I landed a huge bullfrog, fairly hooked in the lip. He had flicked the frog off the lily pad with that whiplash tongue. Several of his relatives were sounding off around the shore, so when it was dark I took a flashlight and a landing net and captured three more. None were as large as the first, but they made a bountiful dinner the next night.

I have developed a variety of ways of presenting hair frogs. Usually I let them float for several seconds before animating them, but sometimes it's best to impart a lot of motion right away, as though the frog saw his peril and was trying to escape.

I remember a long, straight run in Cicero Creek (now it's a lake, courtesy of the Army Corps of Engineers) that was split by a sizeable rock. There was nearly always a bass in the eddy below it. One afternoon, having failed to move a fish from below, I mounted an attack from above. I dropped the frog just above and to one side of the rock and let it drift down a few feet, working it all the time as though the frog were losing ground to the current. No luck. Finally I cast the frog about five feet below and to one side of the rock and immediately began pulling it up the current

George Denny

with big jerks that actually skipped it out of the water. It was too much for that bass. He charged out and missed a strike as I gave the frog a jerk. He turned and missed again and again—three times—then connected on the fourth try.

That fish was no great prize—barely fourteen inches—but his pursuit of that little frog was a sight I'll never forget.

I like hair frogs with a flat, blunt face that angles out over the eye of the hook. Then a sharp jerk will make it plane up and sometimes clear out of the water, with gurgles and bubbles. One of the pleasures of fishing the hair frog is finding new ways to move it in the water. But many times no motion is needed. I've taken fish on a frog that was never moved after the cast. Once I know it had rested at least two minutes because it took me that long to fill and light my pipe. That bass sucked the frog under just as I reached for my rod to begin giving it movement. It was such a gentle little rise I thought it was a fingerling, but it was a small-mouth of better than two pounds, the best fish of the day.

There's one game fish I haven't taken on a hair frog, but I hope to rectify that soon. I mean the striped bass that enrich San Francisco Bay and the countless miles of delta water. I've just moved to that area and haven't had a chance to try it. But I know stripers have been taken on wet flies, and some years ago I read in one of the sporting journals of fantastic striper fishing in Coos Bay, Oregon. The writer reported that he took many fine bass on topwater fly-rod lures. I think they were cork-bodied poppers. He said the natives paid no attention to striped bass. All their angling energies were directed at salmon.

If those Coos Bay stripers will take poppers, their San Francisco Bay cousins should love my hair frogs.

Hair Frogs

Trout of
the Tiny Waters

I was a sadly disadvantaged boy; fourteen years old before I first fished good trout water. And it was on that first day of trout fishing that I literally stumbled into an interest that has possessed me to this moment.

I was walking the bank of the Sturgeon River, in northern Michigan, and in my squeaky-new creel were my first two trout. One was a questionable seven inches (the warden who checked me out that evening frowned and shook his head but handed it back without a word) and the other was an inch longer. I couldn't have been prouder and happier if I had trapped a silver fox, the end ambition of every boy in those days. My rod was steel and nine feet long, and my only concession to what I had heard of the wariness of trout was a three-foot leader. My bluegill hook was baited with a live grasshopper. With that rig I had caught my trout, one brown and one rainbow, and come to think of it, maybe I had some small reason to be proud.

I had caught them by dapping; by crouching back from grassy, undercut banks, lowering the 'hopper, and listening for the rise. That was a deceit I had learned in pursuit of bass and bluegills along the inlets and outlets of the northern Indiana lakes where we summered.

While scouting for another place to dap I stepped into what seemed only a slight depression in the lush meadow grass and found myself thigh deep in cold water. It was a channel about eighteen inches wide. I parted the grass that bridged it and saw that it extended back into the meadow. I was about fifteen feet from the river bank, and I waded down it. Six or seven trout flashed out of their grassy tunnel, over the sandy estuary, and into deep water. And they didn't want to leave that fine hidey-hole; I had to just about kick them out of it. They were as black as the marsh mud. One was at least twelve-inches long.

Why do some memories retain richness and flavor forever? Fifty years later I can see those trout darting over the little fan of sand. I can smell the sulphury gas from the bubbles my wading released. I remember a small cut on the back of my left hand, made by the saw edge of that tough grass. A grasshopper crawled up the front of my waders. I stunned it with a slap and tossed it into the river, where a fine trout had it at once. That splashing rise and the sight of the broad tail as the fish turned back down is still so vivid that, if I were an artist, I could draw it to the tiniest detail. On the other hand, I cannot at this time recall the color of my wife's dress the day we eloped, some ten years later. That is a matter I should not have mentioned and fortunately it was never brought to her attention.

I tried for that trout but my gear was for dapping, not casting. Then I turned back to the secret little stream. I followed it through the meadow and for most of its course it was

Trout of the Tiny Waters

167

hidden by the long grass. There were a few spots where I could lower the 'hopper to its surface. This I did to the best of my ability, but those fish were too shy. Trout in such spots are as jittery as a chipmunk with the hives. They must be scared to survive. They can't flee very far.

They were there. I made sure of that by standing far back from the open spots and tossing them live 'hoppers. They had them instantly; one even jumped a couple of inches to take one from a blade of grass.

About two hundred yards from the river my streamlet disappeared into a marshy thicket too cumbrous to traverse. Then I did a childish, mischievous thing. I waded back the entire length of that little channel, trying to herd all the trout before me, so I could see them flee into the river. But there were wide spots, and even in the narrows I felt fish bump my legs in the muddied water as they darted back to familiar holds. At the end I moved only four or five more into the river. I expect that they, like the first lot, lived near the river and were used to visiting it at times.

And so on my first day of trout fishing was born an interest in trout of small waters, an interest that is even keener today. Now I would know how to try for that trout that leaped for the grasshopper. My gut would be 5X or 6X and my hook short-shanked and not larger than size fourteen. I would approach his pool so carefully my footsteps would not jar the gelatinous ground. The grasshopper would be hooked lightly through the back and kicking strongly as I lowered it to the blade of grass. It would not last long.

Better yet, I would try a dry fly, sparsely tied and no larger than size sixteen, and make it bob and dance a few inches above the water. I think something would have it before it ticked the surface. If that didn't work, I'd lower a small, dark nymph to the

George Denny

168

bottom, let it stay there quietly for a couple of long minutes, then bring it up slowly, with the tiniest of jerks.

Of course if all else fails, there are worms. I remember an opening day many years ago at our fishing camp on the Little South, near Baldwin, Michigan, when all the big waters were too high to wade and too muddy even for streamers. As all trout fishermen know, openings are apt to generate atrocious weather, but that was one of the worst we had ever seen. Our club was not too strict about bait fishing. We didn't ostracize a man for using worms, but he had to sit below the salt and might find he was assigned to the rickety Army cot in the corner farthest from the stove. He certainly would not be invited to participate in our intricate system of pools; the cash awards that were an important part of our outings. We had prizes for the biggest fish, the most fish, and the largest rainbow, brown, and brook. There was also a complicated structure of awards based on the total length of all fish taken, with bonuses for any over twelve inches. Some evenings it took so long to figure out all the prizes there was barely time for the poker game.

Chick Moores, the Oldest Member and the purest purist, let down all bars on that opening day. He remarked at breakfast that since we could fish only the small, brush-lined tributaries, we might as well send to town for a gallon or two of worms and make them legal for all the pools. Agreed. That night we displayed the largest catch that could be remembered for any opening, or any other day, for that matter. We all had limits except one or two diehards who persisted with artificials.

That day my affection for tiny streams paid off. I knew exactly where to go—a nameless meander that drained one swamp into another. It was far back in the woods from the Little South, the river to which its seeps ultimately found their way. I had discovered it while grouse hunting and kept it secret

Trout of the Tiny Waters

169

for a sound reason. It held brook trout, and they were highly prized, having virtually disappeared from the larger waters.

There was an alder thicket shielding a pool on the edge of the upper swamp, and from that tangle the flow entered the meadow. In past years I had cut holes in the branchy curtain. One was still negotiable, and my first cast with a small Black Gnat brought a rise.

Only two or three times have I been able to persuade a trout out of that snaggy area and that was not one of them. After I retrieved my fly from a root I turned to the meadow. The stream there was much like the one I'd found on the Sturgeon, but larger and with more open water. The heavy rains that had so flooded the rivers affected the swamp drainage very little. My streamlet was a bit higher than usual and the water a shade darker.

I dropped the little black fly into the open spots as expertly as I could but had no encouragement except for one short rise. I changed to a small brown nymph, and they liked it. By the time I'd fished the quarter mile of meadow to the lower swamp I had four brook trout and one brown, the first I'd seen there. It was nearly twelve inches long. None of the brooks was more than ten.

As I ate lunch the rains returned, gently at first, then steadily and heavily. That was all the excuse I needed. I fished back through the meadow with worms, mostly dapping, though there were pools large enough to accept a gentle lob cast. I was one short of the limit when I'd covered half the distance. All but one were brooks, and one was the largest I'd ever taken there- —just under fifteen inches. I saved one space in my creel for the pool at the upper swamp. There were big fish there.

I stood at one side of the opening I'd cut and swung the worm through it. Whatever took it after it sank from sight in the

George Denny

170

brown water was too much for me. It tugged and chugged to the back of the pool and far under the roots. I broke the leader, tied on a new hook, and took my last fish from the meadow stretch.

I collected two pools and a couple of bonus awards that evening. My largest brookie won that division and the fourteen picked up the cash for the greatest number of that species. But several browns and rainbows were larger than my best. Chick took first with a brown nineteen inches long. He fished near the mouth of a tributary of the Baldwin that in dry weather was so tiny it harbored only minnows. He reasoned that because of the flood good fish might come into the small stream to escape the heavy flow and have first chance at food scoured down. He kept nothing under eleven inches.

I mention those extreme conditions to show what worms can do in turgid water. They're murder; they should be outlawed. On the other hand, worm fishing in clear water does not appear to be such a killing method. Many times in June or July we saw plunkers—so-called because of the weights they used to get their worms to the bottom—fishless while we scored well with artificials. I recall one exception, but the man was not a plunker. He used no weight, and his leader was long and fine. He lobbed his worm gently upstream into all the good cover along the banks and let it drift back naturally. He had a basket of beauties and was more than a little embarrassed about them.

"Don't often worm fish," he said. "It's my last day and there hasn't been a rise and I promised the kids trout."

Excuse enough, I thought, and I know you're a fly fisherman. That rod is a Payne and barely three ounces.

One summer the meadows along the Boardman River bore a bumper crop of grasshoppers. The bright August days were nearly always windy, and there were stretches where I could walk the windward bank and kick up clouds of 'hoppers. Some

Trout of the Tiny Waters

171

couldn't make it to the far side, especially on slanting reaches, and the water would boil with rises as they ditched. Then I would drop back and fish up with a grasshopper fly tied by the barber in Traverse City, and those chummed trout would race for it. Came the day when friends and family could absorb no more trout, and I was sated to the point of golf. The tiny streams saved me from such heresy. There were plenty of them in that country. One was named Belanger Creek, if memory obliges. It flowed into Grand Traverse Bay about halfway between Traverse City and Northport. A few yards back from the road the brush was nearly impassable, but short of that I caught two keeper browns and a brookie which had to go back. That one spurred me on. I followed the streamlet back, probing for openings where a rod tip could be inserted. After half a mile of struggle I had two more browns and a brook. Above that was a quarter mile of open meadow where I changed from worms to a dry fly. In most cases I had only one cast at the small pools and narrow runs. An attempt to pick up the fly would almost surely snag it in the tough grass. But I caught two brooks and a rainbow before the flow welled from an impossible swamp.

I fished back through the meadow and took two more, a brown and a brook. I made no further attack on the brushy stretch; I was bone weary. I had worked three times as hard for ten fish as for the fifteen taken so easily from the Boardman a couple of days earlier. But four were brooks, and I'll remember them when the easy limits are forgotten.

Halfway between Northport and Leland a tiny rill named Houdek flowed under the road in a culvert and immediately disappeared in a thick woods. That was my next target. The rivulet bored from the open roadside ditch directly under the roots of a cedar tree and out of sight. From then on, all through that forest, it was underground most of the time. I traced its

George Denny

172

course with difficulty. More than once I stepped through the crust of moss and earth that bridged the narrow channel.

On my first reconnoiter through that dim woods I caught no fish, although I carefully lowered a worm into all the promising holes. I didn't expect to, knowing that my quarterings as I puzzled out the course would shake the ground enough to put fish down. Three hours later I retraced my steps and took three brooks and two browns. The most exquisite care was needed in the approach. After failing on the first three or four attempts I tried the waiting game. I sneaked into position as gently as possible, then stood, hardly breathing, for at least five minutes before offering the lure. That was the answer, and from then on I could take those woods trout any time I cared to make the effort. The back and sides of those fish were black, and even their bellies were dark gray.

Montezuma's Well, in the Verde Valley of central Arizona, is the source of most of the flow of Beaver Creek. Above the Well it appeared to be a trickle not worthy of attention and in any case too warm for trout. I had not learned how the desert will soak up and warm streams soon after they flow from the rocky canyons. But Digger, the Hopi Indian, set me straight.

"Go up two, three miles," he said. "Springs up there, cold water. Rocks fall down, make deep pool. Plenty fish."

The last half mile was a scramble, but I finally came to the rock slide. The canyon walls were nearly vertical at that point and the pool only eight or ten feet wide and too deep to wade. I could fish only from the rock dam at its foot, but no more room was needed. Those native trout hit a fly or small spinner the moment it was offered. I am ashamed to say how many I took back to the ranch, but there were no limits in that country in those days on fish or game for the table, and we polished them all off that evening.

Two weeks later I visited that pool again. As I neared the

Trout of the Tiny Waters

place I heard a dull boom and shortly came upon Charley Hollingshead, the deaf old cowpuncher who was homesteading a couple of miles downstream. He was picking up fish as they floated down to the rock dam. They appeared to be stunned. He looked at my fly rod and grinned diffidently.

"Didn't know anybody fished this place," he said. "But the pool ain't hurt. I used less than a half stick of powder. It only got the ones close here. Plenty more farther up and they'll come down soon."

I tried to look severe, and the old man picked up his sack of fish and stumped off down the canyon. That does it, I thought. No more fishing here for a while. But it was time for lunch, and I ate my sandwiches and smoked a leisurely pipe. As I rose to go, a fish broke the surface forty or fifty feet up the pool. That can't be a trout, I thought. Probably a shiner or maybe one of the stunned fish gulping air. But it won't hurt to try.

I rigged up with a small streamer behind a tiny brass spinner. In two casts I had a trout. The next one came harder; I had to reach out as far as I could with the little combination and let it sink deep. Then suddenly, strangely, those trout forgot their fears and I caught them almost as easily as on the first trip.

I reported the dynamiting that evening at the ranch, expecting that others would share my concern. Not so.

"Old Charley needs them worse than you," was the consensus.

Just above timberline in Estes Park, Colorado, is a tiny lake —I can't recall its name or even find it on a map—where trout rise for only a few minutes each day in late summer and early fall. The rise is just after noon and is triggered by clouds that swirl through a gunsight pass and loose a few drops of rain at that time. I was told it happened every day, right on the dot, and there was no use trying for the trout, visible in windrows, until that magic moment. I didn't believe that, of course, and wasted an hour with every

Trout of the Tiny Waters

175

trick I knew while my more experienced companions made coffee and roasted hot dogs.

When the first clouds eddied through the pass the three other fishermen hurried to favorite spots around the shore. I picked a spot where a huge snowbank kept my backcast from snagging. As the first big drops splashed down, those trout went wild. For about ten minutes they hit any lure we threw at them. Then they stopped as though a switch had been pulled. Never before or since have I seen or heard of such a regimented rise.

The four of us then laid out twenty trout, about half brookies and half native cutthroat. The largest wasn't much over ten inches. But the best was to come. That late in the season the outlet of that minature lake was a small flow, but there were many deep pools. It was like fishing down a flight of stairs; the slope was at least twenty degrees. The stream bed was cluttered with huge boulders, and the flow often ran out of sight under the rocky jumble. But where the pools could be reached we caught trout with nymphs and wet flies. They were fine fish, all cutthroats, and they averaged twelve inches. The largest was near sixteen. We all filled our limits.

Under most conditions I concede that trout of the tiny waters can best be taken with bait, but there are ways to do the job with flies and nymphs, and the feeling of achievement is vastly greater. Nymphs are deadly when the knack is learned. As for acquiring that skill, I am now pretty well convinced that years of trial and error is the only way. Hewitt said just about all there is to say on nymph fishing, and I memorized that chapter, but it was long and long before pieces of the puzzle began to fall into place.

For what it's worth, and with a low bow to purists and no apology to plunkers, I have now forsworn bait. No more worms or salmon eggs or hardware. There are not too many fishing trips left. On those I intend to travel first class.

George Denny

Doves

There were lots of doves in my home state of Indiana, but we couldn't hunt them. They were classified as songbirds. That was absurd, of course. Doves do not sing; they complain. And as Father pointed out, it wasn't proper for a songbird to be such delicious eating and, under most conditions, such a wonderfully difficult target. But he was an officer of the court, and he made me obey the law, though he thought it silly and strove to overturn it in the Legislature.

And so it was not until 1949, when we moved to California, that I experienced the delights and chagrins of dove shooting. My first hunt was with Clyde Becker, who lived near Riverside. He took us to a spot called Pigeon Pass, where the birds flew up from their roosts in the valley to feed in the weed and grain fields. There were six of us, and Clyde positioned us across an open field and just under the brow of the hill so we could see the birds as they topped the rise. Dove shooting in California starts thirty minutes before sunrise, so it was still dark as we took our positions. A few birds ghosted by before it was time to shoot, and I could see that this hunt would be an experience. In a few minutes Clyde yelled that it was time, and at that very second a dove flicked into view and came right at me. I missed the incoming shot, and he twisted by not five feet from my head and disappeared into the darkness of the slope behind me. But another and another and still another came into view, and after two or three more misses on those incomers I remembered to raise the barrels to blot out the bird just as I pulled trigger and began to get a fair percentage.

That was dove shooting at its best. They came in singles and doubles with now and then a bunch of as many as five or six. We were far enough apart to safely take shots to the side, but those birds weren't visible in the first light. For a while we could only see the ones that came right at us, and they were tricky, twisty shots. But my wide-open twenty was perfect for that sort of work, and I had my ten birds before sunrise. I won't tell how many shells it took but will admit visiting my car for a second box of twenty-five.

Several of the party were shooting choke-bore duck guns, and they were almost helpless against those low-flying incomers. But when the sun rose they could turn and take them going away, and soon we all had limits. That first dove hunt made me regret all those wasted years when the law said no.

We feasted that night. Clyde fired up the barbecue pit, and by early afternoon rocks were glowing hot in the hardwood ashes. He wrapped the doves in wet burlap sacks together with onions, carrots, celery, potatoes, and a seasoning sauce. He covered the hot rocks and ashes with wet clay, put the sacks on the clay and covered them with more clay and dirt. The pit steamed all afternoon, and when we opened it just before dinner the sacks were still damp and the contents perfectly cooked.

We lined up in the same place the next morning, and this

George Denny

178

time the birds were flying scared. Perhaps they were twisting and ducking more because of a brisk breeze, or maybe they had learned something from the previous morning. In any case it was right sporty shooting, and one or two of the party came up short.

We opened the season at Pigeon Pass for the next three years, and then the inevitable southern California blight struck it. Clyde phoned to tell us sadly that Pigeon Pass was now covered with houses and there would be no more shooting there. From then on we went to the Imperial Valley for our doves, and for the next fifteen years we opened the season there or in Antelope Valley. Those Pigeon Pass hunts are still sharp in my memory. It was always tricky, demanding shooting.

On the other hand my memories of later openings are not so vivid, and I think I know why. It was too easy. On the first day the doves were tame. I've stood in open fields with no attempt at concealment and seen them float gently in and land within a few yards. I've watched them fly toward me across open fields, barely clearing the fences, and as they neared me they swerved only enough to keep from knocking my hat off. Many of those September-first openings were scorchers, and we tried to get our birds early and hightail to cooler parts. Sometimes we had our limit before sunrise.

Strangely, while doves are the number-one game bird in California, most of the shooting is on the first two days of the season. About half the hunters are satisfied with the opening-day action and try no more after that. Some stay for the second day, and that's all for them that year. Not one in fifty hunts after the first week.

This I cannot understand. For my money the last of the season is best. Birds that would fly by in easy range on opening day then veer wildly at the sight of a hunter, and those are times when it's a hunt, not a laugher.

Doves

179

I do recall one opening day in the Imperial Valley when birds were coming to a field of harvested milo. At least thirty hunters stationed themselves in and around that forty acres and made little or no effort to hide. It was no contest. If birds landed out of range, we could usually walk to within fifteen yards or less before they flew. On that morning I got ten birds with eleven shells and was ashamed of the one miss.

Then business reared its ugly head, and it was two weeks before I could return to that field. My son and I were the only hunters that morning. There were about half as many birds, and they were a lot smarter. They came in high and fast, and if we weren't well hidden, they stayed well out of range.

Remembering my success on the opening, I cockily took only the fourteen shells left in the box. When I returned to the car for more ammo an hour later I had three birds and a bruised ego.

In his delightful account of *A Summer on the Test* John Waller Hills used a phrase I will always cherish. In telling of a day when the trout were even more shy and selective than usual he calls the fishing "wonderfully difficult." So it was on the second hunt that year, and I remember several soul-satisfying shots. What I can't recall is the number of shells I fired that day for a total of eight birds, and please, let's speak no more of it.

On one midseason hunt in the Imperial Valley the hot weather persisted, and near noon the heat and humidity were nearly unbearable. Nearby was a concrete irrigation ditch with about fourteen inches of running water. I stripped to underwear shorts, tennis shoes, and hat, and sat in the water, gun in hand and shells on the bank. I needed three more for a limit, and sitting there immersed to my ribs I got them in the next hour. The last one was thoughtful enough to fall in the ditch and float down to me.

Southern California dove hunters are convinced that they

George Denny

180

are, or soon will be, victims of unseasonable weather. If there are a few drops of rain or a chilly night or two just before the opening, they are certain the birds will all have emigrated to Mexico. The same dire forebodings hold for any time after the opening; they are sure the birds will flee south if the weather man looks cross-eyed. I can't subscribe to those defeatist notions. True, some birds are smart enough to get their little fannies out when the cannonading starts, and those in the high deserts are itchy about cold nights, but I've never seen a day of the season in the Imperial Valley when I couldn't get a decent hunt around Niland, Calpatria, or Holtville. Several years ago my son and I found a place where a combination of feed lot, grain and weed fields, and a stand of eucalyptus trees always had birds. They would feed in the morning, then retire to the big trees to rest in the shade until time for the evening meal.

We always had good shooting there; not only during the entire month of September but also in the second part of the split season—the first fifteen days of December. I'm liable to be called a liar for that last statement. Most dove hunters hold that the December season is a stupid waste of time because by then the birds will all be in Mexico. They are wrong. I'll give odds I can go to that aforementioned spot during the December season next fall and if I don't get doves, it will be because they are wary and scary and I can't hit them. They'll be there.

Nine years ago I moved from Pasadena to Jack London's Valley of the Moon, north of San Francisco. One of the first orders of business was to inquire about dove hunting prospects. Predictions were gloomy. There weren't many doves in the valley—that much I could see. I would have to go east to the Sacramento Valley. Furthermore, I would find no open hunting as in the south. I would have to make friends with a rancher or somehow wangle permission. There simply weren't any open shooting areas worth reporting.

Doves

Then I realized how fortunate indeed were those southern Californians. There is virtually no posted land in the best hunting areas. Although the law states that hunters must have written permission from landowners, that provision is never enforced, to the best of my knowledge. That was nine years ago, and I haven't hunted there but once since moving north. Conditions may have changed.

That first year in the Valley of the Moon I could not find time to do much serious prospecting for a spot for the opening, and when that day approached I had no plans. This wouldn't have mattered so much if only my sport had been at stake, but my son and his wife decided at the last moment to drive up from Long Beach and join me for the opening.

I had heard there were doves in the vicinity of Winters, a small town east of Sacramento. We cruised the back roads near there and saw a few birds, but all the land was posted. Finally we went to the town and asked a filling-station operator where we might find a chance for a few shots. He told us to try near the town dump, a mile northwest of town. As we neared the place we heard shooting and saw cars parked along a road that bordered a fig orchard. Doves were flying in all directions. We found a place where we did not conflict with hunters already stationed, and in an hour we had our limits. The birds were crazy for those figs. I've never seen a better concentration, and we noted that they were bigger and fatter than the ones from the Imperial Valley.

That was dumb luck; it wouldn't happen once in a hundred times. We could have been arrested and fined. I do not recommend such a chancy undertaking. I went back to that spot five days later and found it plastered with large, new NO TRE-SPASSING signs.

One of those birds was banded. We sent the little aluminum tag to the proper address in Washington, D. C., and learned that

George Denny

182

the bird had been banded as a nestling that spring within a mile of where we shot it.

If southern California dove hunters can be called jittery about the weather spoiling their fun, I would have to say that the ones up north are positively pathological about it. They are convinced that all their doves will wing away south at the first hint of rain or chill. I've talked to hunters who refused to try on the opening because there had been rain or cold weather. Even if there were a few birds left, they would take off as soon as the shooting started, I was assured.

At first I believed these pessimists and was content with a day or two at the start of the season. But later that fall I saw a number of doves while hunting pheasant and ducks in the Sacramento Valley. I remembered seeing lots of the little mourners during the quail season in Indiana, sometimes when snow was on the ground and the temperature near zero. Was I missing some good shooting? I decided to make my own investigation.

The next summer I found a spot not far from Arbuckle where there were plenty of doves. I paid a small fee for permission to hunt the place, and let me say here and now that I no longer feel that such a pecuniary arrangement detracts from the pleasure of hunting. My father, rest his soul, would have felt his amateur standing besmirched if he had to pay money for permission to hunt, but he spent much time and gasoline cruising the country-side in search of farmers to befriend. I'm sure that the cigars, boxes of candy for wives and children, and other bribes added up to more than the cash fee I paid. And let's face it—the days of free hunting are just about over in most farming and ranching areas. The Imperial Valley and some other spots in southern California are the only exceptions that come to mind.

Having made my arrangements I tried to find a hunting companion. I approached several men, and they all gave me the

Doves

183

same brush-off. Why pay for a one or two day shoot and that doubtful? they said. If the weather continued warm and clear, I might have a good day or two, but that's all I'd get for my money. Thank you, but no thanks.

The opening day was a Monday in the northern half of the state, and that undoubtedly cut way down on the number of hunters. About a dozen showed up at the spot I had chosen: a deserted fig orchard where birds came after feeding in nearby weed and grain fields. When it was time to shoot, thirty minutes before sunrise, we saw doves flying down from roosts in the foothills. Mostly they were too high, but I managed to scratch down a couple before the sun rose. Then for nearly an hour, there was little or no action. A huge mullein field half a mile away swarmed with hunters, and the sport there must have been out-standing. It sounded like an old-fashioned Fourth of July.

About eight o'clock the birds started to come to the orchard. They seemed just as tame as on the opening days in the Imperial Valley. There was no need to hide. I saw two men shoot at one bird. Both missed and he kept coming without even a swerve and landed in a tree not forty feet from me. I felt he'd earned another chance and threw a stick at him and watched him fly away.

I had my birds and was on my way home a few minutes after eight. Several others were leaving at the same time, and if there were any who didn't get a limit there that morning I suggest they take up croquet.

I went back there the following Thursday, arriving about two in the afternoon. There were no doves in the fig trees. A man and his son were parked at the far end of the orchard, and they told me why. The had arrived at noon and found plenty of birds, but they were skittish and took off after a few shots. None had returned.

I knew from a preseason scouting trip that doves did not use

George Denny

184

the orchard in the afternoon. I drove up to the foothills and hunted along a small stream until dusk. It was hard, hot work, but some birds were there, and I got seven. In the morning I was at the orchard in plenty of time, and the opening-day pattern was pretty well repeated. I got one bird before sunrise, it was quiet for an hour, and then they came to the fig trees in bunches. It seemed as though there were as many as on the opening day, but they were a lot scarier and so the sport was better.

To make it short, I returned to that spot four more times that month. I never saw another hunter or heard shots. Each time the birds were smarter, but there were always plenty of them, and they were still coming when I had my limit and was leaving. On the last day of the first part of the split season, September 30, I had my bag and was on the way home at nine-thirty. That was a few minutes longer than it had ever taken before.

I went there once during the second part of the split season—the first two weeks in December. All the leaves had fallen from the fig trees, and this made me pretty sure no doves would come to them. I was right. A couple flew by, and I took one long shot, but that was all and I soon called it quits. As I approached my car and unloaded my gun a big ringneck rooster clattered up about twenty yards away. I stuffed a shell in the right barrel and snapped off a desperation shot. The big boy flinched but recovered and kept climbing while I watched, cursing softly. Then suddenly, a hundred yards out, he collapsed in midair. He was stone dead when I got to him, and later I found only one number eight pellet and that in his neck. A most unlucky bird, but he saved that hunt.

On the way home I stopped at a filling station in Arbuckle and chatted with the attendant. I told him I had seen only two doves, and he agreed they were getting scarce. But they were still there, if one knew where to look, he said. He had shot five the previous morning, and his companion had taken six in an hour's hunt.

I told him of the six good hunts I'd had in September, in spite of predictions to the contrary. He smiled.

"I seldom hunt on the opening," he said. "Too many guns. There are always plenty of birds later on."

"Always?" I asked. "Wasn't this an especially good year? Didn't the weather stay warm longer than usual? Don't the birds all take off at the first bad weather some years?"

He thought for a moment.

"This year was about average. I've lived around here for twenty-two years and hunted every one of them. Maybe two or three of those times we had weather bad enough to drive a lot of the birds out early in the season. Even so, there'd always be some hunting if a man would work at it. If the weather's bad here it's worse up in Washington and Oregon and we get their birds. I've never seen it when there weren't some doves here all winter."

I've learned to seek and value local sporting advice, but if I had done that with those dove hunters mentioned earlier, I would have missed a lot of fine shooting.

This postscript is written several years later. I have to retract some of those kind words I wrote about the Imperial Valley. After an absence of about six years I opened the season there with my son, and conditions had really changed. Large areas are now posted. Furthermore, we had the bad luck to encounter the day when the Valley was the hottest place in the entire United States. It was simply too blazing hot to move. For the first time we didn't take our limits. I think I'll hunt the northern parts of the state from now on.

George Denny

186

Bits and Pieces

Lake Vieux Desert straddles the Michigan-Wisconsin border, and circa 1925 it was known to harbor huge muskellunge. George Green heard of them and decided he must have one. He talked his parents into a two-week stay there, and they invited me. It was mid-August, and we didn't know that was the time muskies are said to shed their teeth. There is no truth in this notion—they shed teeth gradually all year round—but in any case, they can seldom be persuaded to hit a lure or even take live bait during the hottest weather. We learned that from the natives the day we arrived, but we tried hard for a week anyhow. We didn't see a fish, and maybe that was just as well. A big muskie would probably have smashed our light bass tackle.

In the cottage next to us was a man who came home every evening with smallmouth bass. Not just ordinary bass—great big ones. George and I helped him clean them and marveled at their heft. We would have gladly put aside the pursuit of muskies, but the man wouldn't tell us where he caught those fish.

"If I let it out there wouldn't be any left for me next year," he said.

But we must have looked properly wistful and trustworthy because on the last evening of his stay he relented. He handed us a burlap sack and what looked like a butterfly net.

"Go down along the shore and catch two or three dozen of the little grass frogs," he said. "Throw in a few handfuls of wet grass or ferns."

There were plenty of the little frogs, about two inches long when folded. We took about forty back to his cabin, and he showed us how to rig them. He brought out some long-shanked hooks, about size 2/0, with a much smaller hook welded to the inside of the shank just below the eye. He hooked one of the frogs lightly through the lips on the small hook and secured it to the shank of the large hook with a rubber band around the waist. A silver spinner about as large as my thumbnail completed the rig. He got out a map of the district and showed us where to go—a chain of small lakes about fifteen miles away. I can't recall their names.

"You fish the lower lake," he said. "When you rent a boat there they'll try to sign you up for an outboard motor and guide. They'll tell you the only good fishing is far back on the upper lakes. Tell them you just want to row around a little and won't need anything but the boat. And now, this is important. Don't let them see those frogs. Bundle that sack up and hide it in a creel or under a sweater. Row to the far side of the lake and start casting the shoreline. If anyone comes near you, stop fishing with the frog

George Denny

188

rig and use plugs. You won't catch anything with them but don't use the frogs again until there's no one close. By that I mean half a mile. I've had them following me with binoculars. Now, I'm trusting you boys. If I come back next season and find everybody using frog rigs in that lake, I'll know why."

We solemnly promised, and it was all exactly as he had told us. The lake had been dammed to raise the water level about four feet, and that killed trees along the shore. Many had fallen into the lake, and it made cover bass couldn't resist. Nearly every cast into those good-looking spots brought action. We soon learned to put the little ones back, and by little I mean less than three pounds. We returned at least twenty bass, and the six we kept averaged nearly four pounds. One was over five.

That was not an easy secret to keep. We couldn't hide the big string and were questioned closely as we turned in the boat. We lied like good fishermen. We said they were all taken on top-water plugs. I doubt if they believed us.

On the second day we kept only three bass, but they averaged over four pounds. When we showed up on the third day we were followed by two boats and had to use plugs most of the morning. We caught nothing with them, and when our shadowers finally gave us some privacy we went back to the frogs and caught more big bass. By this time we had more than we could use or give away, and we put all but one back. That one was well over five pounds. For five days we enjoyed smallmouth fishing such as I never hope to experience again. The rig was too heavy to cast with a fly rod, but we trolled it slowly along the shore and caught and released bass until we lost count. On the last day George caught the monster. It weighed six pounds six ounces on the camp scales. When I saw that fish I knew the meaning of the term "mossback." The moss on the top of its head was more than an inch long.

Bits and Pieces

And now, sir, wherever you are—the gentleman who trusted us with his secret—I can assure you it has been safe until this moment. I hope there were plenty of bass there for you the next year. I still have one of those big frog hooks you gave me, and I've tried it a few times. I never caught a fish with it anywhere else. And today I wouldn't use that rig even if I could find that chain of lakes again. I can't forget how those little frogs tried to free themselves from that hook. They used their hands. That's the one disagreeable memory of an otherwise happy experience.

A National Park ranger once told me that in nearly forty years of service in parks that were all in mountain lion territory he had never seen one in the flesh. He'd seen plenty of sign, fresh tracks, deer that had been killed by a lion within minutes, but never had he caught a glimpse of one of the big cats. And he added that there were plenty of other rangers and ranchers who would tell the same story.

"There're quite a few of them left but not many people ever see one," he declared.

If what he says is true, I am one lucky man. I have seen three wild mountain lions. One was in the Imperial Valley of California, almost due east of the little town of Calipatria. The lion had been drinking in the Coachella Canal at dusk, and he came up the bank and crossed the road into a swampy thicket not fifty feet in front of our headlights. He was not as large as I had imagined a lion should be, and at first I wasn't sure of what I was seeing. But bobcats don't have long tails, and this pussy did. Witnesses were Ernie Way, my son Roger, and one of Ernie's boys, whose name I can't recall.

The next occasion was several years later, around 1962. I was with my brother-in-law, Paul White, and we had just driven up the mountain road east of Porterville, California, in search of

George Denny

190

morel mushrooms. It was late spring or early summer, too late for morels under normal lowland conditions, but I reasoned that some altitude might set us back seasonally to a time when the little sponges would be popping out

We found no morels, though we carefully explored every thousand feet or so all the way up to where there was still snow. On the way back we hit an unexpected jackpot. It was a twisty mountain road, not too steep, and Paul was drifting quietly along, out of gear, as we rounded a sharp curve. There, in the middle of the road, were two mountain lions. They were not more than a hundred feet away. One was larger and darker than the other, with head and neck almost black. It must have been the male. The lighter, smaller one was surely the female, and I think we had interrupted a courtship.

The big one made one of the most prodigious leaps I have ever seen—at least thirty and possibly forty feet up what seemed to be a sheer wall of rock, on which it must have had a clawhold or two. The smaller one slid gently out of sight down the hill.

We stopped the house-car and stared in awe at the spot where the big cats had just been.

"What a sight," Paul said softly.

"We'll never see the like again," I added.

I hope those kitties got together again soon and made some little mountain lions.

In 1938, give or take a year, Carol Klinger suggested we pool resources for a game dinner. We gathered at Charley Cox's house, and the participants included Chick Moores, Bill Sully, Henry Atkins, Ray Millholland, this reporter, and one or two others. Carol was chef. The wives made biscuits and a salad. Everything else on the table was game we had garnered that fall.

We had a choice of squirrel, rabbit, possum, several varieties

Bits and Pieces

191

of wild duck, plenty of quail both hot and cold, grouse from Michigan, a goose from the Illinois River flyway, Hungarian partridge from the Red Key district of Indiana, woodcock from the Valley of the Anawak, and jacksnipe from Bacon's Slough.

We ate until there was no more room, took a brisk walk to shake it down, came back and ate more. I tried to sample some of each dish but didn't make it. The quail, snipe, ducks, and woodcock were too tempting, and I could only take a longing look at the goose and other goodies. But we were young and hungry, and we battled that huge meal to a standstill. There wasn't enough left for hash. But of course that was B. C. (Before Cholesterol.)

Mention of cholesterol brings to mind a subject that has puzzled me for years. Forgive me if I digress from the general subject of the outdoors and talk about milk for a moment.

How long since you have seen a bottle of milk topped by rich, golden cream? Some time in the late Thirties cream disappeared from our milk in Indianapolis. I've wondered why and asked the question many times. I've never had a satisfactory answer from anyone in the business.

When we were kids the measure of milk was the butterfat content. Dairies with the largest amount got the most business. And there was never any doubt about it; the cream sat right there on top of the bottle for everyone to see and measure. Low-fat or no-fat milk was unheard of, and I'd like to see it that way again. If cream kills me, it will at least be a rich and happy death.

Mother would turn the bottle upside down and shake it to mix the cream with the milk, and nothing sold by the dairies today can compare with it. They tell us their homogenized product has just as much butterfat as in the old days when we could see that golden richness. I don't believe it. I'm sure they got together and worked out that homogenizing dodge so they would no longer

George Denny

192

have to compete with each other in offering the most cream.

And that reminds me of another story about milk. When I was a reporter on the *Indianapolis Times* in the mid-Thirties, our editor, Talcott Powell, got into a splendid hassle with whatever state board or agency policed the dairy industry. He contended that the public had the right to know the bacteria count in their milk. The state officials hit the ceiling. Absolutely, positively no, they said. All the public needed to know was that their milk was safe to drink.

Powell would not be rebuffed by bureaucrats. To the dismay of his business office, who moaned that he would lose them all the dairy ads as well as alienate other business interests, he hired a private laboratory to take the bacteria count of milk from all the local dairies. Each morning, reporters bought milk from the delivery wagons, and it was rushed to the laboratory. Results were printed in the late editions.

I forget the allowable bacteria count, but it was in the order of a maximum of 15,000 per cubic centimeter. When we printed the results it showed that all our milk was safe, but from the public outcry you would have thought the dairies were trying to poison us. Few had ever given a thought to the number of organisms in their milk. But bacteria was a frightening word, and when people realized they were downing tens of thousands of the little beasties in every swallow they didn't stop to consider how they had survived that long; they only feared the next drink would be their last. Many mothers panicked, and some refused to believe the soothing assurances of their pediatricians. Dairies with low bacteria counts were flooded with calls for new business. The ones with higher counts lost customers in droves. Powell's life was threatened in an anonymous letter. It was a mixed-up mess for a while, and may indicate that the less we know about some things, the better.

Bits and Pieces

This happened a few years ago in a like in a public park in Albany, Oregon. I had an hour or so to wait before a business appointment, so I wandered along the shore, admiring the wild ducks that seemed to prefer that welfare-state existence, where the public fed them, to the normal hazards of the wilds. I talked to the park superintendent, and he said only a few were transients, that most of them lived there the year 'round.

As I approached a clump of bushes on the bank, a mother mallard emerged and led a brood of ten or eleven tiny ducklings to the water. The superintendent was delighted.

"Her nest is in there and I've been waiting for the eggs to hatch," he said. "The little ones aren't more than a few hours old."

But as the family took to the water, they were immediately attacked by two large mallard drakes. Those bandits chased the tiny ducklings, grabbed them by the wing or head, and held them under water, apparently trying to drown them. At first the mother was able to chase away the raiders and rescue her youngsters, but the attacks persisted until the brood was scattered to the point where the mother couldn't protect all fronts. To make it worse, a third drake paddled up and joined in the cowardly proceedings.

The superintendent ran to his office and came back with a long-handled net with which he slapped at the drakes and then herded the little ones up on the bank. At this point the hero appeared, or maybe it was the heroine—I can't tell a Canada goose from a gander. In any case, the big bird joined the superintendent in chasing the drakes away, and when the mallard family was safely up on the bank it followed and took a defensive position between them and the water. Two of the drakes tried to climb the bank, but the goose attacked them savagely and drove them back into the pond.

George Denny

194

"Never saw anything like that," said the superintendent. "Looks like that goose will take over and protect them. But just to make sure, I'll build them a chicken-wire pen up on the hill and we'll keep them in it for a while."

This he proceeded to do as I stood a safe distance away with the net, ready to assist the goose if matters got out of hand. I say "safe distance" because that big bird wouldn't allow me within thirty or forty feet of the mallard family. If I tried to get closer, she raised her wings, pointed her long neck at me, and hissed like a basket of snakes.

When the pen was completed we herded the mother mallard and her babies toward it. The goose bit the superintendent on the leg, and I was only able to keep it away from me by strenuous efforts with the net. But while I distracted the big bird the superintendent penned the mallards, and we backed away and left the goose in charge.

A few hours later, with a sack of grain, a couple of slices of bread, and the best intentions in the world, I returned to see what had developed. The big goose was right in front of the pen, staring at me with a baleful eye. As I got within about fifty feet it took off and flew at me down the slope—beak and long neck pointed directly at me—and hissing loudly. At the last moment I ducked to one side, then ran. I'll admit to being more than a little frightened. I couldn't get close enough to throw the food into the pen; not with that splendid guardian on the alert. I went to the superintendent's office and gave him the grain and bread. He said he would get the food to the mallards.

"That big so-and-so chased me off a little while ago," he said. "I'll have to figure some way to outsmart it. I'll have one of the boys let the goose chase him while I run up in back and toss them the food."

"Ever see anything like this before?" I asked.

Bits and Pieces

195

"Never," he said. "I've seen cats nurse baby rabbits and a rabbit take care of a baby squirrel, but a Canada goose trying to adopt a family of mallards—that's a new one. You know, I think those damn drakes were trying to kill and eat the little ducks. Never saw that before, either."

I told the story to my business associate, Frank Vandenburgh, and he promised to follow it up for me. A couple of months later he reported that all the mallards were fine and back in the pond and able to take care of themselves, and the goose just looked in on them now and then to make sure all was well.

Since writing the above I have talked to another park superintendent where there are a lot of wild ducks. He had seen the same thing happen and has another theory.

"I don't think those drakes were trying to eat the little ones," he said. "They wanted to drown them so they could persuade the mother to start another family. Just a bunch of sex fiends."

In 1910 I saw Halley's comet. Grandfather took me out on his front porch and showed me where to look. The sun had just set, and the comet was following it down. The head was bright, and the long tail faded to nothing.

"Take a good look and don't forget it," he said. "You'll probably never see it again."

"Why not?" I wanted to know.

"Because it won't be back for seventy-six years," he said. "That will be nineteen eighty-six."

I stopped smoking six years ago. I may fool the old gentleman yet.

We know about the marks hoboes and gypsies used to put on front gates to tell the next transient what to expect. Hence the phrase "easy mark" for houses where handouts could be had

George Denny

196

without chopping wood or other distasteful chores. That was many years ago, before welfare and other assists made it unnecessary for the very poor to beg for a living.

Now I'm sure that animals have the same system. No stray dog ever passed us by. They would pause at our front walk, a spark of hope would light their weary eyes, and they would come straight to our front porch and demand food and shelter. Since my family has always considered dogs equal to most people and superior to some, they were seldom disappointed. We couldn't take them all in, of course, but if unable to find their owners we nourished them until they were able to resume their wanderings.

It was the same with cats except that they came down the alley and applied at the back door. My daughter loved cats and always invited them in for a snack. Sometimes this was resented by the resident dogs, and I recall one frantic moment when a feline visitor was arched and spitting on the sideboard and the dogs barking treed.

For years we had a cat called Beeball, short for Butterball. She had offspring at every opportunity, and our semi-annual kitten clearances were sad affairs, with the children crying to keep them all. Beeball finally wore out and was replaced by Fluffy, a daughter. Fluffy had just as many kittens but was more choosy about her lovers. She preferred Persians, so her children had a certain distinction and were easier to give away. We had other cats, but I can recall the name of only one. Would you believe Sweet Baby Doe?

I'm not sure this anecdote has a place in this book, but to me it is so amusing I would like to use it if my editors approve. Maybe we can sneak it in on the excuse that the chief character was one of God's little creatures, a squirrel.

Bits and Pieces

The story concerns James Whitcomb Riley, the Hoosier poet, famous for efforts like "Little Orphant Annie" and poems with such deathless lines as "When the frost is on the pumpkin and the fodder's in the shock."—poems for children, mostly, though he was reputed to dislike the little monsters and never married or had any kids of his own.

It was told many years ago at the round table of the Indianapolis Press Club by Micky McCarty, then executive editor of the *Indianapolis News*, and heard there and repeated to me by Jamieson Campaigne, then an editorial writer for the Indianapolis *Star* and now chief editorial writer for the New York *Daily News*. At third hand it may lose some verity, but I have tried not to embellish it past a reasonable point.

As a celebrity, Riley was much in demand at civic and social functions and was expected to say a few words at such times. So much so, in fact, that he felt he was being imposed on and decided to call a halt to the practice. He was a positive character, was James Whitcomb Riley, especially when in his cups, and that, I am told, was more than occasionally.

Came the time when a most important banquet was planned —an occasion that would include all the influential folk in Indianapolis. Riley was asked to speak. He refused.

"I've sung for my supper for the last time," he said.

Fervent pleas failed to move him, and the sponsors finally had to agree that he would not be asked to talk but simply must grace the affair with his presence. Riley accepted with that understanding.

Riley showed up more than a little sloshed. He was seated at the head table. After dinner and a speech or two, the toastmaster, knowing he had the man at his mercy, said, "And now we will have a word from our distinguished poet, James Whitcomb Riley."

George Denny

Riley was furious, but he hid it well. He rose slowly, twirling his pince-nez from the black ribbon from which they always hung, faced the august assembly, and spoke approximately as follows:

"Ladies and gentlemen, I am not prepared to make you much of a speech because I was told I would not be called on."—He paused, glared at the toastmaster, and resumed—"But I will say a few words; very few. I want to tell you about the problems of trying to make a living by writing poetry. Sometimes the Muse deserts me for days, weeks, or even months. I have recently been through such a sterile period, and it was most difficult. But by great good fortune, just this morning I had an inspiration and was able to compose a short piece—just a couplet—two lines. I rather like them and want to share them with you. They are as follows:

> The higher the little squirrel climbs the tree,
> The smaller his asshole seems to be.

Then Riley bowed, turned, and made his way slowly and with great dignity from the banquet hall.

Owen O'Dell was the son of the minister and my best friend. The summer we were eleven our parents gave us reluctant permission to test our Boy Scout ambitions and skills. We had just about memorized the Scout manual and were confident we could survive in any wilderness. We took bedrolls, cooking kits, and some canned goods. Dr. O'Dell drove us in his Reo touring car to Corydon, a town near the Ohio River, and turned us loose.

Ownie had just read Major's *Bears of Blue River,* and we explored in that direction. Soon we came to Wyandotte Cave and spent days wandering its miles of passages. Our guide was the son

Bits and Pieces

199

of the owner, and he took us into sections that had never been explored. We didn't have sense enough to fear getting lost, and once we crawled for hundreds of feet through tunnels that sometimes pinched down to ten or twelve inches. Today I would expire in claustrophobic terror in such a spot.

We camped on the banks of Blue River in a beautifully wild stretch that was rich with smallmouth bass. We had no rods—only hooks and lines—but we made do with willow poles and caught those bass on any bait that was handy—worms, grubs, or grasshoppers. We cooked them over hardwood coals and seasoned them with salt and hunger.

It took us four days to hike home with some assists from trucks or tourists. One hot noon we detoured to take a dip in a cool creek, and from its banks we flushed the first ruffed grouse we had ever seen. At first I thought it might be a wild turkey. Once a thunderstorm threatened as evening approached, and we sought permission to take cover in a barn. The farmer's wife noted our scrawny condition and fed us fried chicken until we could hold no more. She bedded us down in a spare room and sent us on our way after an enormous breakfast, and with canteens full of warm, fresh milk.

Not far from home, hunger overcame our high principles, and we stole and ate a number of cantaloupes, known as mushmelons in those days. They were little things, not much bigger than a healthy orange, but sweet as honey. Why don't melons taste as good now? Why doesn't anything taste as good now?

After we stuffed ourselves our consciences took over and we went to the farmhouse, admitted all, and offered to pay. The farmer frowned fiercely and demanded a nickel from each of us. Then he cranked up his Ford and drove us the rest of the way home. Said he had to go to town anyhow. Had some tradin' to do.

George Denny

200

Two or three years later I was one of about twenty Boy Scouts recruited to pick apples in an orchard on the bank of the Ohio River not far from the Blue River area. World War I was raging, and all the regular apple pickers were over there chasing Kaiser Bill. One of my clearest memories of those two weeks is the apple fights. We would chose sides and assail each other with three-foot limber switches with an apple impaled on the sharpened point. It was a formidable weapon. A whiplike throw would propel the apple long distances at high velocity. I remember wondering how I had lived so many years ignorant of this splendid weapon. About twenty years later I introduced the sport to my sons, and they were just as pleased. Their mother was not.

There were catfish and white perch in the big river, and we caught them on set lines. The land tortoises were new to most of us. We scratched our names and the date on the shells and turned them loose with some vague hope we might find them many years later.

The nearest town was Solon, a hamlet of very few inhabitants. Today I can't even find it on a map, and I expect it has withered away and lost its post office. But I recall one thing about it with crystal clarity. In the town square was the town pump, and to the pump there was attached, by a chain, the town toothbrush.

Now in all honesty I cannot say whether that was a public toothbrush or the property of one citizen, or maybe one family, whose rights to it were respected by their neighbors. And it did not occur to me to ask the question that would shed light on this delightful bit of bucolic custom. More on this subject in a moment.

About fifteen years later my wife and I visited that same southern Indiana country in company with Gilbert Hurty and his intended, Phoebe Craig. Gilbert had never been on safari, but he knew his elephant sign. We were chugging our way down a gravel road not far from the town of Marengo when the huge droppings loomed up ahead. Gilbert finally broke the awed silence.

"Improbable as it may seem, I will state with some conviction that an elephant has recently passed this way," he said.

Sure enough, when we approached Marengo a few minutes later a small one-elephant circus was raising a tent on the edge of town. And the next morning as we strolled the town square I saw it again; a toothbrush chained to the town pump, just like the one I had seen in Solon.

Gilbert was entranced. He improvised, paraphrased, and chanted something along these lines:

> "The old village toothbrush,
> The moss-covered toothbrush,
> The iron-chained toothbrush
> That hung by the well."

The Canal

The water company canal had an important part in our young lives. It was built during the canal boom of the nineteenth century and was a part of what was to be called the Central Canal, a two-hundred mile stretch that would connect with other waterways and ultimately extend from the Great Lakes to the Ohio River. But the railroads put an end to that dream, and the water company bought the short section that ran from the Broad Ripple dam, north of the city, down to the settling and purification ponds near the heart of town.

The water company didn't like us to swim in its canal, but that was a difficult rule to enforce. We could spot the guard walking the towpath in plenty of time to dress and scatter. Fishing was frowned on, although the company must have known that this was asking a lot of small boys. The guard would usually look the other way. We caught small mud cats and bluegills and those brilliant little sunfish called punkinseeds. Now and then someone would hook a good channel cat or bass.

When I acquired a new piece of fishing gear I would test it on the canal. I remember one Sunday morning when I was trying one of the weight-forward fly lines that were new in those days. I rigged up with a small hair frog and worked it just outside the weeds along the bank. The smallmouth that took it was the best fish I ever hooked in the canal. He was just under fifteen inches, and he fought me hard. At the height of the struggle, services ended in a church across the street, and in no time I had an audience. One deaconish type began to give me advice.

"Stop fooling around with that fish and pull him in," he admonished. "That's a good one. Pull him in."

I assured the gentleman I way doing my best, but he didn't understand fly rods. It was several more minutes before that bass gave up.

The best sport we had on the canal was jugging. We would rig up a dozen or so glass jars or bottles with weighted lines and hooks, bait them, throw them in the canal, and follow as they floated down. When a fish took the bait, the bottle would zigzag in the current and might even be pulled back against it. We would man both banks, and sooner or later the bottle would come close enough to one so we could snare it with a gaff.

That was an exciting way to fish, much better than sitting on the bank with a pole or even fly fishing. But when the water company discovered what we were doing it had a corporate conniption fit. Fishing with a pole they might overlook, but this new method was too much. They issued stern injunctions, and after a couple of us had been marched home by the ear and given a final warning in the presence of parents, we gave it up.

For the twelve years before we moved from Indianapolis to California we lived within five minutes walk of the canal. Before World War II the water company crews kept the towpath bank clear of weeds and bushes, and I fished with a fly rod by walking

George Denny

204

the towpath slowly, against the current, and trolling a fly and spinner or streamer fly just outside the water weeds along the bank. But during the manpower shortage of the war the bank was not kept trimmed, and weeds and bushes grew so high I could no longer angle in that lazy manner.

One day in July of 1947 I walked down to the canal to see if the vegetation had been cleared from the bank. It hadn't. In places it was shoulder high and hung out two or three feet over the water. It was not comfortable fly fishing, and I soon gave it up and sat on the bank. Many years ago I learned that if I was perfectly quiet for a while the wild things would forget about me and go about their business.

In a minute or two a small turtle came from some cover along the bank and paddled slowly toward a tiny crawdad that was nibbling minute forage on a strand of weed. The little crustacean whirled around and faced the threat with his nippers open, then flipped his tail and shot out of sight. The turtle surfaced for air, and we stared at each other for a long minute. Then he dove to the bottom in about four inches of water and began to rake the mud with his claws. In a moment he ducked his head and came up with some sort of larva in his beak. He chomped that morsel thoughtfully for a minute, then began to search for another.

A V in the water near the far bank told of a muskrat swimming against the current. It climbed out on a small log, sat up, and preened like a cat. Soon the sleek wet fur was fluffed out. A bluejay swooped down to investigate, decided the muskrat was harmless, and went off without a word.

About this time I became conscious of a small disturbance by the towpath bank about fifty or sixty feet upstream. Little ripples and splashes were coming out from under the overhanging vegetation. I tried to imagine what caused them—a

The Canal

mink or coon hunting frogs or a bass chasing minnows in the shallows?

The ripples moved slowly toward me with the current. I picked a spot where I was well hidden by the brush but could see down to the water's edge. When the little ripples were about ten feet away I saw what caused them. A wood-duck hen with six tiny ducklings. They were hunting insects in the over-hanging grass and diving for larvae in the shallows.

I held my breath as they worked down to a spot directly below me. Then mama sensed danger. She cocked her head, and one bright eye looked up at me. She uttered a faint warning, fluttered out from the bank, and headed across the canal. The youngsters followed, paddling madly and flapping tiny wings. Their efforts were enough to get them up on their tails, like little hydroplanes, and they skittered across and dived into weeds on the far bank.

I reported the incident in my outdoor column in one of the daily papers, and the moment I saw it in print I was sorry. I feared some game hog or thoughtless kids might harm my ducks. I am happy to report that such was not the case. I watched them brood until they were grown enough to fly, and mama raised five of the six; a fine percentage.

There was another brood in the same place the following year; almost certainly the same mother. There were twelve little ones this time, and she raised all but two. I never saw the elegant male duck or found the hollow tree where the mother made her nest.

Years ago I shot a wood duck. Three of them jumped from a small stream, and I fired through a screen of leaves, not knowing what they were. I downed a male and have regretted it ever since. They are simply too beautiful to kill.

George Denny

206

The Artful Dodger

Father said the only way he ever downed a jacksnipe was by accident.

"There's no way to figure which way they'll zig or zag," he complained. "All I do is fire in their general direction and pray. Sometimes an unlucky one will twist into the pattern." Actually, that's a pretty fair summing up of the problem of jacksnipe shooting. I can think of no bird with a more erratic flight. There's no graceful curve to the flight when a snipe decides to change direction after the rise. It's literally a sharp, jerky angling, like that of a bat whose radar has just locked onto a beetle way off to the side somewhere.

When I was breaking in on rabbits and quail I would occasionally jump a jacksnipe or two. I was even more of a snapshooter then than I am now, and I wasted a lot of lead by blazing away right after the rise. After too many of those misses I learned to hold my fire until the little corkscrewers got the first couple of twists out of their system, and then I began to get my share. And though there are only a couple of bites of dark meat on their little breasts, I rate them the most delicious of any game bird I ever tasted—better even than quail or woodcock.

I've heard there are areas where jacksnipe hunts can be planned with a reasonable hope that birds may be found. I've not been fortunate enough to locate one of those spots. That rasping *scaipe* as they jump has nearly always been a happy surprise. There have been minor exceptions. I gradually learned enough about where they use so that I could expect to kick a few out when conditions seemed right. There was a swampy area known as Bacon's Slough near the city. We often jumped ducks from its potholes, and I found snipe there often enough so that I would usually load the right barrel with a light load of eights or nines. It was there I learned that nines will kill a big mallard drake as surely as sixes; I think even more surely at reasonable ranges when the head and neck are exposed to the pattern.

I learned something else at Bacon's Slough. One day after a clean miss at a snipe, I idly watched its flight. After the preliminary gymnastics it climbed and curved almost out of sight, then turned back and dived into the grass not fifteen yards from where it had jumped. I can't recall whether I made the second chance good, but from then on I always watched carefully to see if the little perishers turned and came back, and I found that they did a reasonable percentage of the time. And they glide back and dive into the grass so smoothly and quickly one has to watch closely to see them. I hate to think how many chances I missed before I began to look for that return.

George Denny

208

When I left Indiana for southern California I sadly said goodby to bob white, woodcock and, I thought, jacksnipe. I couldn't imagine the little boghoppers in that hot, dry country. My first duck hunt with Clyde Becker corrected that misconception.

The blinds were in the middle of a valley in the low hills southeast of Riverside, on the banks of a series of shallow ponds. There were six of us in four blinds that morning, as I recall. I don't remember much about the early stages of that hunt except that there were not many ducks. Clyde made a lovely double on two that did wander by, and I believe those were all we got. What bugged my eyes out were the jacksnipe.

At first I didn't believe it. When Clyde flushed one as he left the blind to get his ducks I thought it was just one of those nameless little wading birds, though the twisty flight seemed familiar. It wasn't until he jumped another on the way back that I was sure. This time I heard the rusty-gate *scaipe,* and there could be no doubt.

When no more ducks showed in the hour after sunrise, we called it quits. As we walked to the cars parked half a mile away I got Clyde to one side and told him we must find an excuse to go back to the ponds after the others had left. As we got into my car he announced loudly that he had forgotten his pipe. They pulled away, and I drove back and parked a discreet distance from the ponds.

"Now what's this all about?" Clyde wanted to know.

"Jacksnipe," I said. "Lots of them."

"Jacksnipe?" he asked.

"I saw eight or ten," I said. "You kicked a couple out when you went for your ducks. As we left the blinds a lot more jumped. Didn't you see them? I was sure one of the others would spot them and start shooting."

The Artful Dodger

"I doubt if they would know one anymore than I," Clyde said. "Are they fair game?"

"They are back in Indiana. They must be here, too."

"What are we waiting for?"

By some great stroke of luck I had been too lazy to put away the low-base shells left over from the dove season. There were a box and a half in the trunk, and those light loads of nines were perfect for snipe. Clyde had to make do with duck loads. There were at least forty snipe around those ponds, and they wouldn't leave the only water in miles. They flew from one pond to another, and I'll bet we missed some of them four or five times. It was the only time I ever had a chance to take a limit of snipe, and I finally did it, although I began to wonder if the shells would hold out. Clyde did as well, though handicapped by duck loads. It was a memorable hunt.

I couldn't get back to those ponds that season, and when I visited them the next year they were dry and there was nary a snipe. I've never found another such concentration to this day.

Still to Do

I read somewhere not long ago of a sporting expedition for billionaires. A travel agent proposed a year-long cruise on a yacht; a trip designed to put participants in the right place at the right time for the finest hunting and fishing the world has to offer. No detail was overlooked. There would be professionals to advise and teach, and their gun and tackle shops would be fully stocked. The first stop would be Iceland for the salmon of the Laxa rivers. Then to Norway for sea trout and salmon, England to fish the Test and Itchen, and Scotland for the red grouse. In the winter they would go to Africa, South America, and New Zealand. No price was mentioned, perhaps on the J. P. Morgan principle that if one needed to know how much it cost to maintain a yacht, one could not afford one.

I put that prospectus aside with mixed feelings. Who would have the time and money for such an adventure? Probably some wheezy, old plutocrats who wouldn't know a nail knot from a double Turle or a jacksnipe from a woodcock. Better the trip be funded by some foundation or sportsmen's group that would send lean and hungry men like me—men who would properly relish it. So went my envious musings.

But the thought stayed with me, and I've mulled it over many times. Given unlimited time and money, where would I go, what would I do? As I write this, it is the middle of September. If I could start that trip tomorrow, I would go to the prairies of Saskatchewan. Nowhere on this continent is there a greater wealth and variety of wildfowl, and it's a junket I've dreamed of for years. There I would get my first Canada goose and one, or maybe a brace, of those noble birds would be enough. I would especially want a few of the grain-fed mallards and the tender little teal. Those last are what they call "breakfast ducks" on the Eastern Shore, and that's the time to enjoy them. Teal are not difficult when jumped from potholes, but I would like to earn them fairly, downing them with an unbelievable lead as they rocketed down wind.

There would be Hungarian partridge and pheasant and sharp-tailed grouse. Forget the ringnecks; they can be found in many places and to my mind are not difficult targets. I would try hard for the sharp-tails. I think I have seen them only once, many years ago, from a train crossing the northern prairies, but those may have been prairie chickens.

I would know the Huns. We had a few in Indiana, and Bill Sully located them and took me to them back in the Thirties. We found a small covey—small as Hun coveys go—not more than thirty birds. They flushed far ahead of the dogs. We marked them down a long quarter of a mile ahead, and the

George Denny

212

singles held pretty well to point. We got two apiece, as I recall. One I can't forget. We were working a fence row, and the bird came out on my side. I snapped off a shot that was fairly long for the twenty double, and the bird towered, up and up in tight circles, at least a hundred yards. I had seen quail tower after a head shot but none nearly as high. That bird dropped dead at my feet, and the impact split the skin on its fat breast.

There are grouse and woodcock in Saskatchewan, but I would save those hunts for the Baldwin area in Michigan where the grouse made me look so helpless years ago. I know there are jacksnipe there as well. If the fishing season was still open, I would surely wet a line, and even if it wasn't, it would be good to revisit the Clay Hole and High Banks and Sheep Ranch and the Octogon Castle stretch, and each spot would remind me of some angling victory or defeat.

It was near the High Banks that I walked a woods trail some forty years ago and heard an animal climbing the steep slope just ahead. I stopped and watched a doe top the rise, and she was followed by a fawn that couldn't have been more than two or three days old. She saw me and snorted and bounced into the brush with her baby right on her heels. And then, a few seconds later, a second fawn appeared and stood in the path and looked about for its mother. It saw me and bleated like a lamb and came toward me as though to say, "I'm lost, help me." I think the little thing would have come up and nuzzled me, and that I did not want to happen for fear my scent might alienate it from its mother. I backed away, and then the doe returned and stood in the path and stamped hard twice. The fawn bleated happily and raced away after her.

Somewhere in my development from a young savage to a reasoning, civilized adult there came a time when I no longer wanted to kill a deer, or any four-footed animal. Now I think it

Still To Do

213

was on that long-ago morning on the woods trail when the tiny fawn approached me so trustingly.

Back to my dream trip. I would spend the best days of Indian summer in my native state of Indiana. First I would go to Little Tippecanoe Lake, where I caught my first bass more than a half century ago. I expect it would be so built up and civilized that I wouldn't recognize it, but the channel to Big Tippecanoe would still be there, and it would remind me of the day I first saw a fly rod used. I would search those reeds and lily pads with a hair frog for old times' sake. And if the marshy channel to Lake Webster was still navigable, I would pole through it hoping to jump a mallard or a teal and possibly a jacksnipe. I would take the fly rod because I remember a place where the narrow channel widened into a pond ringed with lily pads, and under them lived some huge largemouths. I didn't have any luck with them when I was a boy, because I hadn't the patience to wait for half an hour, or even longer, until those old mossbacks had forgotten the ripples made by my boat as it entered their pool. I've learned patience, and maybe I could outwit one of them now.

If the hazy, lazy Indian summer days continued and autumn rains held off, I would try for smallmouth bass at some of the places I fished thirty or forty years ago. Late-fall fishing is often the best of the year. The Tippecanoe River stretch where I caught my first bass on a fly rod is now Freeman Lake, but below the dam and before the Tippecanoe enters the Wabash there should be some wadeable stretches that would remind me of that day. A few miles farther down, in the big Wabash, there was a wide and comparatively shallow spot pocked with rocks and rich with runs and scours that always held bass. It was tricky wading, and I remember more than one fall on the slippery ledges, but the rewards were more than enough for that

George Denny

214

risk. If the water looked promising, I would try to find that place. The Wabash used to shelter more big bass than any river in the state.

Then I would go to the place we called Seven Springs, on Sugar Creek. That was a lovely spot; a stand of hardwood untouched for so many years it was beginning to look like the forest the first settlers found in the early eighteen hundreds. Thirty years ago when I last saw the place it was still clean and uncluttered by trash or tin cans. The few of us who went there were so awed by its cathedral-like majesty that we dared not desecrate it. I would hope to find it still unspoiled and with the brooklet formed by the springs full of watercress. And I remember that the smallmouth in that length of Sugar Creek usually took kindly to my fly-rod lures.

Seven Springs would remind me of a coon hunt many years ago. Carol Klinger phoned to say that a waning moon would rise about nine o'clock and we should be afield before then. We had four hounds that night—the blue-tick, Buck, who had the richest, deepest night voice I ever heard; Bess, the black-and-tan bitch that was silent until the quarry treed; and two of Bess's pups, whose names I can't recall. It was a pup that first made game in a cornfield, and a moment later Buck confirmed the find and assured us it was indeed a coon and a hot trail, too. But that one got away by swimming the creek. We found the dogs checked on the bank and ordered them across, but they could not find that trail again.

Then the moon came up—the hunter's moon—so different from the harvest moon, that warm, soft hussy made for the easy pleasance of Indian summer. The November moon was cold and bright and sharp as a scimitar. The night was still, and mist rose in the lowlands and scent hung high. We started seven coons and treed four and left them all unhurt for future hunts. It was

Still To Do

215

a memorable night, and I want at least one or two more like it.

After Seven Springs, weather permitting, I would try a few more of those Indiana smallmouth streams. Big Walnut, Cornstalk, Raccoon Creek, Flat Rock, Brandywine, and Blue River were some of the best. But even thirty or forty years ago they were beginning to be damaged by pollution, and now I would hope for the best and fear the worst. When we have laws that put the big polluters in jail and keep them there for a few years we may see some improvement. Short of that I see little hope for our environment.

But the fishing would just be marking time for the opening of the bobwhite season; to my mind quail hunting is the greatest upland sport of them all. I would have two dogs—a fast pointer to search far out for the coveys and a slow setter bitch for the singles. I would hope for a singles dog as sure and steady as our old Ruby, but that may be asking too much. I doubt if I will ever again see her equal.

I would not get my fill of quail hunting in Indiana and would follow the season down through Kentucky and Tennessee and into the Carolinas and possibly Georgia. Archibald Rutledge wrote so enticingly of his Santee River delta country that I must see it and try for a few of his ducks. Even more important would be the hope of a chance at my first wild turkey. One would be enough.

Three months of bird hunting would bring me to the midwinter doldrums when trout fishermen begin to count the days to the opening. I would be only a skip and a jump from the riches of the Florida Keys and that would be my next move. Father left me a nine-and-one-half-foot bamboo rod I have never used. Its backbone has not been needed in my pursuit of bass and trout, but the bonefish, tarpon, snook, and other battlers of the Florida waters would surely test it well. And I'd

George Denny

like to try for permit. Only a few dozen anglers have taken that prize on a fly rod. I don't know what makes me think I might have a chance to join that select group, but as long as I was in permit waters I would try.

Time would fly as I fished those abundant Florida shoals, and as May first neared I would have to decide where to open the trout season. I have never fished the eastern streams and those famous names—Beaverkill, Brodhead, Neversink—would tempt strongly. And since I recently reread John Waller Hills's *A Summer on the Test* I would give thought to a trip to England. But I'm sure nostalgia would carry the day, and I would choose to open the season in Michigan on the streams of the Baldwin district that I used to know so well. The weather would probably be atrocious, as usual, and the fishing poor, but there would be the familiar stretches and the hope that an old-timer or two like Doc Crane or Whit Clapsaddle or Bill Sully might remember me and we could reminisce over a beaker or two of strong waters. That would bless the trip, weather or no.

Then I would try those eastern trout streams. Much of their best stretches are private or owned by clubs, but if I looked wistful and promised to fish only with barbless hooks and put everything back, maybe someone would have mercy. I might even dare impose on Alfred W. Miller (Sparse Grey Hackle), with whom I have carried on a sporadic correspondence. Many years ago when we had some minor business dealing he took me to the Angler's Club in New York and even suggested that he might be able to arrange a weekend at Hewitt's camp on the Neversink. I can't recall what I felt was important enough to make me decline that opportunity; I can only admit it was the stupidest decision I ever made. Short of direct intervention by the Almighty I should have gone. It would have made a priceless addition to these memories.

Still To Do

217

After learning all I could in those hard-fished eastern streams I would head for the Nipigon. We don't hear much about that river these days, but it surely holds brook trout much larger than I have ever taken, and I want a chance at them. A five-pounder would make me a happy angler.

Then I would find a bush pilot to take me far north to waters holding the Arctic grayling. I hear they take small dry flies eagerly and their silver and turquoise iridescence rates them among the showiest of all fresh-water prizes.

The next stop would be Alaska, where there are streams with summer steelhead to twenty pounds and more. They can be taken on dry flies, and a few encounters with their like would be something to remember.

In mid-August I would go to Campbell River on Vancouver Island, where anglers come from all over the world each season to troll for king salmon off the river's mouth. I don't care for the heavy tackle necessary for those big fish, but I would try it once or twice if for no other reason than to make obeisance to the local angling deities. But the chief reason for that visit would be to fish the Campbell River that Roderick L. Haig-Brown has described so faithfully in his books. Many years ago I wrote a review of his *A River Never Sleeps*. It gave me more enjoyment than any fishing book I ever read, and I said so in loud, clear tones. Haig-Brown was kind enough to write me a graceful thank-you note and invite me to fish the Campbell with him if ever I should get there. I still have that invitation and will surely cash it some day.

At the Campbell River I would look for the harvest cut-throats and the summer steelheads and if the cohos weren't in fresh-water, they might be found in the estuary. I would try faithfully for all of them in the pools and holds that Haig-Brown has described so well, and if I had the great good fortune to watch him fish them for a few hours, my pleasure would be redoubled.

George Denny

218

That would round out the first year of my sporting hegira, and I have planned it carefully. From then on I would proceed as the mood and the season dictated. I have seen a few whitewing dove but never bagged one, and a trip to Arizona would fill that bill. On the way back I would drive up through Prescott and down the long slope through Jerome, the ghost town, and into the Verde Valley. That would be a sentimental journey. I helped build the Rimrock dude ranch there in 1927 and 1928. If the ducks still fly down Beaver Creek just before sunup after spending the night in Montezuma's Well, I would try for them again. That was my first pass shooting, and I burned a lot of powder before learning to give them the necessary lead.

Many consider Atlantic salmon fishing the finest fly-rod sport of all, and I would find that out for myself on rivers with those sonorous names like Cascapedia and Matapedia and Restigouche and Upsalquitch. When I think of salmon I remember the three plates of salmon flies in Mary Orvis Marbury's *Favorite Flies*. There were six to a plate, eighteen in all, and gentlemen, those were splendid creations. Not Solomon in all his glory was arrayed like one of those. I got the book out to refresh my memory of their beauty. I compared them with the salmon flies in the current Orvis catalogue. It was no contest. Those flies tied back in the eighteen nineties made today's specimens look drab. No doubt their brilliance appealed more to fishermen than to fish, and possibly the current patterns are more effective. No matter, I would like to have all eighteen of those flies exactly as shown in those old plates. I would frame and hang them in my den. Durham Ranger, The Notion, Kennedy, Silver Doctor, Popham, Childers, Thunder and Lightening—they are gorgeous.

I would go to Africa for its vastly underrated fishing and wildfowling. I have no desire to do more than observe the big-game animals. If forced to decide between shooting an elephant and some of the miserable humans I have known, I believe I would spare the elephant.

New Zealand, Chile, and Argentina would demand two or three winter months. Surely in some of their waters are trout larger than any taken on a fly rod, and every cast would carry that hope. And at the very least I might allow myself to wish for one larger than I have ever taken. A ten-pound brown, carefully stalked and brought to action with a well-presented fly, then skillfully handled on light tackle—a man can dream.

I've always wanted to see a bustard. In England the last ones were killed about 1870, but there are still a few in Spain and Portugal. Strangely, as I write this, the morning paper tells of an attempt to reintroduce the great bustard to England. Two cocks and four hens have been taken from Portugal to a protected site near Salisbury. But I want to see the big birds in their wild state, and for that I will go to Spain or Portugal. Just to look, not shoot.

Another reason for a visit to Spain is Las Marismas. That is a huge swampland in the south, not far from Gibraltar. All I know about it is what I read in James A. Michener's *Iberia*, but that is plenty. He describes the place in meticulous detail—an area of about eight-hundred square miles, a retreat for countless birds and many kinds of animals. Only in the winter is the entire area flooded. By midsummer great stretches are dry enough to drive over in an auto. Aquatic birds come from all parts of the Continent and Africa, some to nest in the spring, others to wait out the winter before returning to northern nesting grounds. In such a wealth of waterfowl I might be permitted to unlimber the twenty double and hope for a specimen or two new to me. But the main purpose of the visit would be to observe and marvel.

The first order of business in England would be what remains of Walton and Cotton's Fishing-House on the Dove, in Derbyshire. It is correct to use capitals in that spelling, for the place is a

George Denny

220

shrine to any trout fisherman interested in the origins of his sport. I would start that pilgrimage by coming down the hill that so frightened Viator. Cotton called it Hanson Toot, and it's a name one wouldn't forget. Then I'd follow the river down to the Fishing-House and Pike Pool. And one would have to catch a trout from Dove; any little trout would do. There might be a curse on all future angling efforts if one didn't.

Somewhere, long ago, I read that one of the angling clubs in England had blackballed a Prince of Wales because the members knew His Royal Highness really cared little for the sport. That may have been the Houghton Club on the Test at Stockbridge, and I would like to fish there more than anywhere else in this world. It is possibly the most jealously preserved water you can name, so my hope might be difficult to realize. But surely, somehow, I might at least wangle permission to watch the members fish. That would be almost as satisfying. Hewitt was the best we could enter in the international angling lists, and he was humbled by the English chalk streams. He wrote that the Test and Itchen waters were the most difficult and demanding he had ever fished; much more so than any he had tried on this continent.

There are many more fine trout streams there than the three already named. Kennet, Wye, Durwent, Frome, and Nar are ones that come to mind. And I would try the little streams named by Theakston in his book, *A List of the Natural Flies That Are Taken by Trout, Grayling and Smelt In the Streams of Nipon*. I would fish them with flies dressed in faithful imitation of the artificials shown on Plate VIII of the book. That and the seven plates of natural flies and insects are as well done as the ones in Ronalds's *Entomology*, although they're not in color.

It would take more than one summer and fall to get my fill of hunting and fishing in England, Scotland, and Ireland. In Scotland I would put aside rod and gun for a day or so to play the Old

Course at Saint Andrews. It is as much a shrine for golfers as is Fishing-House for anglers.

A branch of my family once lived in County Cork, and they surely fished the Blackwater, Lee, and Brandon rivers and their tributaries. And not far to the north is the River Shannon, and all proper Irishmen must try for a salmon from those sweet-flowing waters.

The shotgun would see a lot of action in Ireland. There are ducks, geese, woodcock, snipe, pheasant, plover, pigeon, and curlew. A brace of two of the ducks and geese would be enough, but I would like to spend a lot of time with the smaller birds. It occurs to me that my enthusiasm for wildfowling is in inverse proportion to the size of the bird. Father drilled into us that we should never shoot more than we could eat. So for years I have been limiting my bag to a few of the larger birds each fall while thinking nothing of downing several limits of dove or quail. An even better reason is that I get a lot more shooting, and a mean, twisty shot that drops a snipe or woodcock is more satisfying than an easy chance at a lumbering goose.

Grouse shooting on the Scottish moors would give me an excuse to shop for guns in London. That is a pleasure I have looked forward to since I began to appreciate the workmanship in fine doubles. Names like Churchill, Boss, Holland and Holland, Greener, Purdey occur to me. I would make myself a nuisance in those shops. To be able to go into any one of them and order a matched pair of twelve-gauge doubles without worrying about the cost—that is my measure of enough wealth. And while I was at it I would be tailored for a twenty-eight-gauge double. It's enough for dove and snipe and the other little ones.

On that high note let this dream end.

George Denny

222